As a Man Thinks
in His Heart So is He

Edward L. Morales

As a Man Thinks in His Heart So is He

Proverbs 23:7

Trilogy Christian Publishers

A Wholly Owned Subsidary of Trinity Broadcasting Network

2442 Michelle Drive

Tustin, CA 92780

For information, address Trilogy Christian Publishing Rights Department, 2442 Michelle Drive, Tustin, CA 92780.

Trilogy Christian Publishing/ TBN and colophon are trademarks of Trinity Broadcasting Network.

For information about special discounts for bulk purchases, please contact Trilogy Christian Publishing.

10 9 8 7 6 5 4 3 2 1

Library of Congress Cataloging-in-Publication Data is available.

ISBN: 979-8-89041-712-1

ISBN: 979-8-89041-713-8

As a Man Thinks
in His Heart So is He

TABLE OF CONTENTS

The Set Up

Defining Terms

Grace: Grace is God, or a person, giving you something you do not deserve.

Mercy: Mercy is God, or a person, not giving you what you do deserve.

Love: Love contains mercy or grace in it most times, love is the giving and exercise of joy, peace, patient, kindness, goodness, faithfulness, gentleness, self-control. If the Spirit of God is love then the fruit of it is as well. Love can be selfless and sacrificial, often love has a cost to the giver, like it did with Christ willing crucifixion, a sacrificial gift from the Father.

2 Thessalonians 1:3, Jeremiah 31:3, Galatians 5:21-23, 1 Corinthians 16:14.

Repentance: is defined as a "Change of your mind" in the Strong's concordance. Repentance is the changing of the way you think and live. God is not interested so much in your "I'm sorry" being verbalized. What He wants is a change of thought and thus a change of life which reveals God's living word working, living, thriving in you. **Psalms 119:9** His goodness drives you to repentance and change of thought and way. You choosing His way over your own way, this equals Repentance a change of mind to His way of thinking this is why **"as a man thinks in his heart so is he"** in his actions. This lesson is all about a renewed repentance, a renewed thinking, a revival of His mind in you and thus His will coming down from heaven and working in you on earth. Please ponder this a bit. Read **James 1:22-25, and Psalms 119:9** both reveal a struggle between the study and looking into the mirror the word and obedience. Here is when you yield and choose Christ and His Cross it is the death of your self-nature.

Salvation: Salvation is intact when you, the bride, have accepted the Groom's proposal to trust in His work for your Salvation. His gift of everlasting life that He freely provides to all who ask Him, requires your acceptance of the gift. Salvation is a trust and surrender to the Lord King Jesus our savior nothing more. He has done the work, no man can add or subtract from His work, no one can steal you from His hand. No man can do it another way so that they should not be able to boast. Now you have laid down your own self-sufficiency in preference to choosing Christ by your own submission and trust and reliance in His work of the Cross and work of Atonement of our Fathers plan. The Father gave you HIS gift of His Son freely because He First Loved us. **John 3:16,** O Father how pleasant and amazing is your enduring love. We live forever discovering its Glory and Praising you my Father for the gift of your expressed love, your Son Jesus Christ our Lord.

Discipleship: It is a cooperative work of you yielding to the Spirit of God. It Is the process of your surrender of your own heart and ways. It is the effort to be His to be a student and study Christ and His ways. **Psalms 1 and 119,** Your submission of will and trust in Him is in exchange for the gift of love and eternal life, it is a response to His first LOVE. **Isaiah 55:8-9** Some confuse discipleship and salvation but they are two different things, you can be saved and not be a disciple. From a Hebrew temple perspective Salvation is in the outer court. But discipleship is in the inner court. **I Peter 2:5-9, NKJV** Pickup your cross and lay down your own life means to lay down the self-life willingly give it to the Jesus and surrender your heart and will to His ways.

Faith: is a deep dependent reliant, trust, it is required because you cannot see Salvation, touch it or feel it but in your heart you somehow KNOW it is. You live by Faith a dependent posture of your mind will and emotions unto Him. You now begin to become aware of the Fathers Love for you ever more deeply in discipleship mode. **Jeremiah 31:3, NKJV.**

Eternal Life:

John 17:3, NKJV,

"and this is eternal life, that they may know You, the only true God, and Jesus Christ whom You have sent."

We ought to teach folks to know and love God first, via prayer and study life and show and model the How to do it. If this is eternal Life knowing and loving Him our Father, why not start now? Knowing the anointed savior and the Father that sent Him is an eternal study and discovery we will thrive and learn from Him forever. It seems to me that who you are today you take with you at the end into eternity. Eternity really starts now today, this is why the urgent call by Paul's expression "now is the accepted time for salvation" and renewed thinking, a repentance to His ways of thinking.

You will find in this lesson that God tells those that call themselves after His name, to do the following, in this order:

1. **Love God** with your whole heart, mind, and soul. **Matthew 22:37-40, NKJV,** This is marked number one because you will need this to be dominant in you, to do the next three, for without Him you can do no-thing of eternal value. Your most valued asset God has ever given you, is your TIME. Spend it well.

   Deuteronomy 11:1,13-15,22-23 NKJV,

   Therefore you shall love the Lord your God, and keep His charge, His statutes, His judgments, and His commandments always. V13 And it shall be that if you

earnestly obey My commandments which I command you today, to love the Lord your God and serve Him with all your heart and with all your soul, 14 then I will give you the rain for your land in its season, the early rain and the latter rain, that you may gather in your grain, your new wine, and your oil. 15 And I will send grass in your fields for your livestock, that you may eat and be filled." V22 For if you carefully keep all these commandments which I command you to do—**to love the Lord your God, to walk in all His ways, and to hold fast to Him— 23 then the Lord will drive out all these nations from before you, and you will dispossess greater and mightier nations than yourselves.**

If I am not in His word or in prayer, *How can I know His ways?* You must make time for prayer and the study of the word which results in a relationship with Him.

When you place yourself in the position, "I can do NO-thing without Him" this is the dependent posture of the overcomer in Christ **1 John 4:4,5:5 NKJV**, the child of Christ **Romans 8:17**, the sons of God **Romans 9:26** that He is looking for in you. Read **John 5:19 and John 15:5, AMP,** The real testimony of Myself in the end is that it has always been Jesus empowering me and giving me breath to live and do, ponder this? I am just a vapor a swirl of dust. The good and faithful servant is the one that has learned to yield to Him, his master. This is why all the glory goes to Him and Him alone. Saints, don't touch the glory ever. This will prove out going forward in your Christian life, pay attention to it. Abide in the vine, for without Him I can do no-thing **John 15:5, NKJV,** of eternal value, but with Him, I can do all things through Christ that strengthens me. **Philippians 4:13, NKJV,** So you see, it has always been about Christ the anointed one in you the hope of Glory and not you. This is why we do not touch the glory; it is His alone. This is why we give Him away and not ourselves.

2. **Love your Christian Brother. 1 John 4:20 NKJV** People inside of Christ.
3. **Love your Neighbor. Matthew 19:19 NKJV** People outside of Christ
4. **Love your Enemies. Matthew 5:44 NKJV** Jesus loved the unbelievers the Roman governing leaders and troops and the Pharisee's and Sadducees of His day and we should love todays misguided governing leaders and religious leaders that fight against the Lord's ways. We must love because God so loved the world. Be a priest and pray for those that you disagree with. **Revelation 1:6,5:10, NKJV.**

This leaves no one out, you must LOVE everyone.
How are you doing so far?

Ephesians 6:12, NKJV

12 For we do not wrestle against flesh and blood, but against principalities, against powers, against the rulers of the darkness of this age, against spiritual hosts of wickedness in the heavenly places.

1 John 4:20 AMP

If anyone says, "I love God," and hates (works against) his [Christian] brother he is a liar; for the one who does not love his brother whom he has seen, cannot love God whom he has not seen.

It has become obvious to me after pondering on these two verses. My fight is in the spiritual realms and not with flesh and blood: people. You cannot hate your brother if you say you love God. A pastor recently said "if you don't love people, you don't love God." Because He first loved us. God overlooks your faults while you were a sinner and in error, He gave you His grace, wooing you, why don't you give out the same Grace to others? If God is in you, then you must respond as He would have responded and give grace to the unworthy sinner. Love, mercy and grace is given to the unaware person and ignorant sinner? This undeserved behavior equals grace, God, or you, giving something to someone they did not deserve. God is LOVE and love shall remain forever, why not learn to love God's way now? Now is the time for salvation and a renewed mind of Christ in you, now is the time!

Sowing and Reaping

We will now focus on the concept of Sowing and Reaping for a bit because of the impact it has on your life and the Life of the church, mostly unaware by the individual. The law of sowing and reaping is elementary essential concept in every person's life weather you believe it or not. It is working in us all. Belief is not required, it is a law like the sun rise and sets and rain falls from the sky to the earth, it just is. From the beginning God wanted folks to INCREASE in everything even today God wants you to share, bear fruit, seed and increase growing in His kingdom influence. **Genesis 1:28** I am not talking about greed of money even though that it is not exempt, I am talking about influence and increasing the kingdom of God with disciple souls these are everlasting treasures we invest in havens account, the hearts of men. **Genesis 26:12-14, Matthew 28:19, Isaiah 54:2, NKJV.**

Matthew 7:12 (AMP)

12 "So then, in everything treat others the same way you want them to treat you, for this is [the essence of] the Law and the [writings of the] Prophets.

Here is a principle of sowing and reaping; **doing** as you want **done** unto you it is a motivational tool of God. Many ignorantly will live life and later reap the consequential fruits of our foolish sinful behavior. We have all done this knowingly or unknowingly. Think on this, husbands and wives what are you lacking in your marriage, then sow it yourself into your mate, run to be first, don't wait. Your harvest is waiting! Love her first, forgive her quickly, adore her first, run and run faster to sow seed and reap a harvest.

Be first to be kind, be loving, be full of joy and you will reap multiplied in return. If I sow seed in my wife she will multiply it and give it back to me even babes are born this way. If I treat my wife poorly then I will reap the same multiplied. Wives respect and allow your husbands to lead. Wives that won't submit are doing the same with God. If you're a man you get double duty, you have to love and sacrifice for your wife and learn to submit to God and His ways.

Sow seed, give out what you want to reap from God and others. You will see this in God's word over and over again said many different ways. Sowing and reaping is not always connected to money but more importantly to relationships.

The law and the prophet's principals are hidden in the concept of sowing and reaping. Again, the truth that we should act and treat others as God advises us in these verses because of the Bible verse Galatians 6:7.

Galatians 6:7-9, NKJV, proclaims:

[7] Do not be deceived, God is not mocked; for whatever a man sows, that he will also reap. [8] For he who sows to his flesh will of the flesh reap corruption, but he who sows to the Spirit will of the Spirit reap everlasting life. [9] And let us not grow weary while doing good, for in due season we shall reap if we do not lose heart.

Read all the Proverbs and Jesus's teachings and think on the concept of sowing and reaping while doing so. You will see the concept of sowing and reaping repeated over and over again. Understanding and embracing the concept of sowing and reaping is wisdom. Sowing and reaping are working in our lives with or without our own intentional efforts. In the natural, if I plant a good garlic clove in good soil soon I will reap garlic cloves but multiplied, they are called, garlic bulbs. My wife and I were farmers of garlic once upon a time in Wyoming. I can plant one clove and get back an increase anywhere from three to twelve or more cloves depending on variety. So, it is with God's Law, words and deeds brings the increase sown in the hearts of men or in the earth, so it is in the spiritual realm. If I sow love in others, then I will reap love multiplied in return, do you see it? **Matthew 13:7-9**, **Genesis 26:12-14, NKJV.**

Luke 6:35-37 (NKJV)

35 But love your enemies, do good, and lend, hoping for nothing in return; and your reward will be great, and you will be sons of the Most High. For He is kind to the unthankful and evil. 36 Therefore be merciful, just as your Father also is merciful. 37 "Judge not, and you shall not be judged. Condemn not, and you shall not be condemned. Forgive, and you will be forgiven.

Look at verse 35-37. Jesus is speaking and reveals sowing and reaping again "the reward is great," He says. We must be kind as He is kind to the unthankful and evil, devilish people in our lives. Are you willing? Sowing mercy and grace, not being antagonistic to one another but caring for the ignorant soul that lacks understanding of God's ways. When I am rejected by others, I brush off my feet and leave in love within my heart for them and pray for illumination of truth in them, help me Lord not to take offence.

I am almost sure that Jesus said this verse 37 because the disciples walked around bickering and condemning one another all the time and finger pointing out the lack and deficiencies in one another, sounds familiar? As a parent haven't you seen this with your children? Haven't you seen this on the internet. At one time or another, we all have fallen to this sin and have been the unthankful and evil ones and He forgave us. v35 Whatever I want from others or from God, that is very thing I should sow in the lives of others. I focus on this concept with my mind and thoughts on Jesus, focused on Him and not on the screaming

As a Man Thinks in His Heart So is He

self-nature in me that wants to be offended. He leads me to still waters in troubled times to refresh me. Blessed is He.

Jesus said "if you do it unto one of these you have done it unto me." When I give mercy and grace to others I have sown it for my later reaping from Him and from others. Remember the law of **Galatians 6:7 and Matthew 7:12.** Try this for a bit remember you plant seeds and they grow to bear fruit, it is not instant. Write it down in a journal see it unfold before your eyes because we often forget seeds planted grow over time like garlic can take over nine months to harvest. Understand this, if you are doing this all the time, then you are always reaping from something you sown earlier good or bad, pick one. Sowing and reaping works outside of faith in it, it is a law, trusting in God is not required for it to function in your life. Inside or outside of Christ you will reap what you have sown! **Galatians 6:7.**

As a Man Thinks in His Heart So is He

Sitting in the Wrong Seat

James 5:9 (NKJV)

Do not grumble against one another, brethren, lest you be condemned. Behold, the Judge is standing at the door!

Don't be found setting in His seat. This is so violated these day because the anonymous way we live. One lives on social media we can slam someone and not care and unaware we have sown it in our own lives. A famous preacher of the 1970's said, "It is the Holy Spirit that convicts, and Jesus is the one and only to judge we on earth are to live in love with one another."

James 4:12 (AMP)

12 There is only one Lawgiver and Judge, the One who is able to save and to destroy [the one God who has the absolute power of life and death]; but who are you to [hypocritically or self-righteously] pass judgment on your neighbor?

O Lord, may I never sit in your seat that belongs to you alone, the Throne of Judgement but let me sit at your feet, O God, and know thee. Help me never be the critic of another soul but if and when I see lack in my brother, let me befriend them and lovingly plant seeds of truth for growth leading them to you. I pray that we all would look to His word for guidance and follow these instructions. Jesus is at the door, do not let Him catch you sitting in His seat, for He is the Lawgiver and Judge alone. James is a book of discipleship and this verse is very sharp, ponder this a bit…

John 3:17 (AMP)

For God did not send the Son into the world to judge and condemn the world [that is, to initiate the final judgment of the world], but that the world might be saved through Him. Read Luke 9:56 (NKJV)

Again, many of us love **John 3:16** we all should but we neglect the very next verse **John 3:17**. And as Christians, we should attempt to be like Christ, should we not? In **John 20:21** Jesus sends us out into the world as the Father sent Him into this world. So, you will not be God nor judge or condemn but rather live in faith like He did, in a dependent posture like He did and have the same motivations with the same mission as He did, to do the will of the Father who sent Him, just like He did. "Our Mission if you wish to accept it:" Is to reach into the darkness of this world and bring others into His marvelous light, to give the world a better understanding of God that results in salvation of the soul. He came to SAVE the world! Not to judge or condemn it at this time. Judgement will happen, but later in the future. Jesus came to be a priest and lamb 2000 years ago until to today. He will soon be the Groom and fetch His bride and later He comes to be a Lion and King. As King He will judge folks but this is not the present dispensation of today, we are sent out to be reconcilers, redeemers, restorers, rebuilders, and wise lambs to win as many as we can and snatch them from the gates of hell, the gates of ignorance, the gates of error, the gates of darkness and broken dysfunction. Today is the dispensation of grace of His holy mercy and love unto salvation. **John 3:17, Luke 9:56 (NKJV)** Hurry Saints, and snatch those that are lost around you!

Treasure Wisdom

Why does God say in **Hosea 4:6, NKJV, "My People Perish from a lack of knowledge"** and understanding. When we leave His concepts and principles like sowing and reaping, we stray from His narrow path, this is why we feel we are alone without His presence and we get poor results in our Christian lives. The good news is "He leaves the ninety-nine to find the one that strayed from the flock" when you go off into error. The Holy Spirit leads you back into all truth if you are seeking Him sincerely. He has done this for me many of times. But when you take off on our own you will get lumps, burrs, scratches and maybe bitten and devoured by wolves, it's no picnic.

We do the leaving; He does not leave us ever, even if you sin, think on this. We depart from the narrow path of principals of His word then we scratch our heads and say, what went wrong? We may not feel like He is with us while suffering consequences but he is. His word says, "I will never leave you nor forsake you." **Hebrews 13:5** He is faithful even when we are not. Wisdom seems to me, to not be a thing obtained but it is more about your heart condition towards God. In Matthew 5, NKJV, wisdom is not listed but the way to get it is, meekness which translates to teachableness in Greek is wisdom. So, learn to be teachable do not ever think your way is the only way. One thing for sure I have learned in my Christian walk if you put God in a box, He jumps out. He will not allow us to confine Him with our human thinking. **Isaiah 55:8-9** reveals His way of thinking.

Proverbs 16:16 (NKJV)

"Get wisdom and in all your getting get Understanding"

You want wisdom? Pray and ask God for illumination read one chapter a day from the book of Proverbs is a good start. Thirty-one chapters for thirty-one days. One chapter for everyday of the month, God's wisdom is waiting for you. Every month start over until it sticks.

Here is a nugget to keep, always run back to read and study **Psalms 1** Highlight that in your Bible and make it an anchor verse, He made this the foundational psalm number 1 the first psalm that a Christian should be built on. This is the first psalm it is the cornerstone and the foundation, Jesus Himself is in it. Seek it out with repetition and to return to it like thirst seeking out a water source, ponder this chapter, because here thrives wisdom. Psalms 119:9-16 and Psalm 1 are conformation and companion verse of one another and point you to maturity in Christ and gives you the "how to" do it. Read it mark it and make it an anchor. **Psalms 119:1-16,33-48.**

Proverbs 12:15 (NKJV)

The way of a fool is right in his own eyes, but he who heeds counsel is wise.

My friends if you think you are wise or Godly, you have already become a fool, but if you know that you lack and have need of Him and His understanding by hungering for God and for His wisdom, you have become wise. Let me teach you something I had to learn myself over the years.

In the Garden of Eden there are two trees, the tree of good and evil and the tree of life. God told Adam not to eat from the tree of good and evil. Here is God saying that very thing to us today. Read **Genesis 2:17.**

As a Man Thinks in His Heart So is He

The Tree of Good and Evil

A person eats from the tree of good and evil, his works maybe evil but his desire is to make those evil works appear good to himself and justified to others. Remember Cain and Abel in Genesis 4? Think about all the sin in our nation and the workers of it, they seek to justify it, to say it is good. Satan appeals to the 'I' in us, the self-nature in us referred to as sarx in the Greek meaning flesh nature like in the book of Romans. His attempt to get us to veer off the path, looking for self-seeking self-benefit. **Genesis 3:4-5.** When Jesus was in the desert being tempted by Satan, Satan appealed to the self-nature in Christ, Satan's target was the 'I' in Jesus to get Him to SIN, remember in the middle of sin is 'I.'

So, here is a man living with his girlfriend sleeping with her, so he will say to himself, *love is from God and I love her so I am good.* The tree of good and evil is a tree were the eater seeks to justify his evil actions as good or Godly. Just as Adam and Eve did. His statements sound good maybe even look good like the fruit but he forgets that the How one does a thing is important to God. Even today many call evil things good and good things evil. God's ways verses sinful ways are vastly different in makeup. **Read Isaiah 55:8-9 NKJV,** But from this tree of good and evil only sin, death, separation, broken dysfunction thrives here. The Adam and Eve story, both of them wanted to make what they did good by justifying their sinful actions. Satan appealed to the 'I' in Eve. Eve ought to have replied to Satan, "You shall live by every word that comes from the mouth of God" then obeyed her own retort and not eat. God said do not eat from this evil tree of good and evil. This tree is available in the hearts and minds of every soul on earth today. We are born eating from the wrong tree, sin. Look at your kids for a moment, you ask them, "Why did you do that to your brother?" Pay attention and see for yourself, the first thing they say, they justify their evil actions immediately, to be good. They are eating from the tree of good and evil. Do you see it now? A patrolman will tell you that everyone they put in the back seat of their unit, will seek out to justify their lawless endeavors with their mouth on the way to jail. Just as an FYI they record everything that happens in the back seat, I was in law enforcement for ten years as well.

The Tree of Life

We need the written word of God to live in our hearts like in Psalms 1 and 119. This means you will have to open that book and study it. I use the word STUDY and not the word read for a reason. When Satan tempted Christ, Jesus defended his actions or inaction by the word of God He had hidden and studied in His heart previously meditating on it. He did Psalms 1 and 119. God's word should be like a filter and a sword, an offensive tool unto us against Satan wiles. As life and situations become present, we respond and act as the Word filter allows us to act and respond. The word is an offensive tool a sword. As you learn to wield the sword it sends temptation running and non-biblical thinking on its way. Because without Him you can do no-thing **John 15:4-5** but with Him you can do ALL things. He is the word. **Philippians 4:13.**

The wisdom is in the trusting in HIM the relying on Him and His word, the dependency on Him, abiding in Him and the truth that delivers me from my own ignorance is found in HIM and in His word. Jesus is the word and He wants to be the answer to your every question! Will you allow it? Will you seek Him out? **Psalms 1,** Will you meditate on His word? Seek Him out like a thirsty panting deer for water. Ask Him to help you to develop this desire. **John 1:1-5.**

Proverbs 21:2 (NKJV)

Every way of a man is right in his own eyes, But the Lord weighs the hearts.

When you grind down the gospel and the Bible it is about the response of your heart and mind to Him loving you, and His word exposing you one on one of all your sins and lack resulting in the awareness and discovery of your need for Him and His ways. Think and ponder this a bit. If you do not understand this above comment, ask God for understanding right now, do not throw it out.

Think on this, as you walk with Him and in His truth the word living in you, the word exposes your sin, one on one with you, isn't that true? YES. Does He proclaim your sin on the roof tops or on the internet? No. Does He share it with others? No. Does He desire to see you fail? No. Does He expose you and your stuff and embarrasses you in front of others? No. We ought to do the same with others. To act even as He acts. We all think we are right, or we would correct ourselves would we not? We even try to make evil things look good eating from the good and evil tree. So every man thinks he is right in his own eyes, even me. The trick is to live humbly before Him and inside yourself, remind yourself your need for Him always, for without Him you are doomed. This is abiding in the VINE of **John 15:4-5**. It is a realization of your inability to live rightly before Him without Him and His word living in you, God Himself. We are dead without Him because He is Life, we are lost without Him because He is the way, we are ignorant without Him for He is the truth. Only with Him do we realize victories in this Life that result in everlasting Glory for Him and Him alone.

John 15:4-5 (NKJV)

4 Abide in Me, and I in you. As the branch cannot bear fruit of itself, unless it abides in the vine, neither can you, unless you abide in Me. 5 "I am the vine, you are the branches. He who abides in Me, and I in him, bears much fruit; for without Me you can do nothing.

How do I Abide in Him?: Abide in me, Jesus says, Live, thrive, increase in my word He says, understand my principals He says, allow Gods word in your heart to become alive and instant in the opportune moment! He and His word becomes your friend, filter and source of our responses to life around us. **John 1:1-5** Jesus is the word. **Psalms 18:30 AMP** Without Him you cannot bear eternal fruit and without Him you can do no-thing. **John 5:30, John 15:4-5,** But with Him I can do all things, responding to Life via the word that is alive in me and you, we can bear good fruit with increase in Him and for Him, because of Him to Him be the Glory forevermore. **Philippians 4:13, Psalms 1:1-6.**

Psalms 18:30 (AMP)

As for God, His way is blameless. The word of the Lord is tested [it is perfect, it is faultless]; He is a shield to all who take refuge in Him.

We thrive and when we teach ourselves to love the word and teach others to learn to love and trust the word of God as well. The logos written word lives in us then, Christ via the spirit makes alive and powerful the Rhema word [in Greek] in you, in a particular situation with assurance it was Him. This is how we hear from God and get Godly results. The walk of Faith the walk of a dependent posture upon Christ as He re-speaks His living word too us.

Romans 10:17 (NKJV)

So then faith comes by hearing, and hearing by the word of God.

Over twenty years ago, the Lord led me to look up the word "hearing" in Hebrew I was attempting to seek out how Jewish folks think about this word "to hear." I was blown away by the concept the word *shama*, in the simplest terms, means 'to hear.' It means to hear, to listen, to give attention, to understand, to submit to, and to **obey**. *So, to hear is to obey* I thought to myself.

So, I rewrote **Romans 10:17** for my better understanding and I will share it here with you. Yes, I know Romans 10:17 is in the Greek but go with me a bit, don't trip. "Faith comes by obedience and obedience to the re-spoken word of God made alive in you in a particular moment or situation." God is looking for instant yielded, action to Him in the moment and in doing so faith will grow and grow in you because you end up being more dependent upon Gods voice the author of your faith to lead you and guide you in all things making Him the finisher of your faith as well. Everything begins and ends with Him the Author and finisher the beginning and the end this is why He gets the glory. Never touch it. **Deuteronomy 4:1, 7:12, 11:1, 28:1, Luke 9:35 (AMP)**

James 1:22-25 (NKJV)

22 But be doers of the word, and not hearers only, deceiving yourselves. 23 For if anyone is a hearer of the word and not a doer, he is like a man observing his natural face in a mirror; 24 for he observes himself, goes away, and immediately forgets what kind of man he was. 25 But he who looks into the perfect law of liberty and continues in it, and is not a forgetful hearer but a doer of the work, this one will be blessed in what he does.

Luke 9:35, AMP

" …This is my beloved SON, My Chosen one; "Listen and obey and yield to Him!" Father says unto us. Think on this a bit. Then reread what I wrote above can you see it?

Below you see how valued the word of God and His precepts are to the writer of this Psalms 119. Listen to wisdom spoken here. The Father gives us a clue, faith is listening and obeying and yielding to Him the logos word living in you. The more we do it the more we grow in faith and flourish, we increase in dependence and reliance because He is the source of all things. If we give our source Jesus away, we give eternal life away, love and liberty to the recipient. If we give ourselves away to others, we give death even though it may look good and not evil, but remember the tree.

Psalms 119:9,11,15-16 (NKJV)

9 How can a young man cleanse his way? By taking heed according to Your word.

11 Your word I have hidden in my heart, That I might not sin against You.

15 I will meditate on Your precepts, And contemplate Your ways.

16 I will delight myself in Your statutes; I will not forget Your word.

Take Heed, "I have hidden, meditate, contemplate, delight myself and I do not forget." All action words for believers in Christ to work on, oh no! Requirements and works? Discipleship is a yielded and surrendered life of obedience unto Christ. This is discipleship the inner court of the temple of God. Salvation is given to all that trust and rely upon Him freely nothing can be added to His work, it is finished; this is the outer court of the temple of God. Keep this in mind salvation is free, but discipleship and His discipline is for the willing surrendered heart to Him and it will cost you your self-nature. He prunes the vines; He disciplines the ones He loves It is a different than and more than salvation. I will get into the temple later in this writing hang on.

John 14:23 (NKJV)

Jesus answered and said to him, "If anyone loves Me, he will keep My word; and My Father will love him, and We will come to him and make Our home with him.

May the Lord make His word thrive, alive and powerful in your life and allow the Word to be understood and become alive in you. May you hunger for the tree of life and eat from its branches. I pray that everyone that reads this book, that they would step out into faith trusting yielded actions in Him because of the word made alive in you by Him and your study of Him the word. The results will amaze you, His kingdom of yielded obedient saints is coming. The bride is being readied, their garments are being readied even now. Read **Isaiah 61:10, Revelation 3:5,18 16:15 (NKJV)**

As a Man Thinks in His Heart So is He

Revival of the Restored

James 5:19-20 (AMP)

19 My brothers and sisters, if anyone among you strays from the truth and falls into error and [another] one turns him back [to God], 20 let the [latter] one know that the one who has turned a sinner from the error of his way will save that one's soul from death and cover a multitude of sins [that is, obtain the pardon of the many sins committed, by the one who has been restored].

Here is God using a person to bring back a lost lamb to the flock from the darkness of error. **James 3:13, AMP,** We are his hands and feet sometimes we go fetch the one from the ninety-nine that was lost. If we can save one from error, we have done a good work. But restoring a brother is a delicate matter. Humility and love should be in the heart of the restorer. Blessed are the peace makers with God and with Man. **Matthew 5:9,** Strive, pursue peace with all people and seek out Holiness, for without which no one will see God for He is Holy. **Hebrews 12:14,** When we were lost without salvation, we were ignorant of the love of God had for us, then over time we understood His great love and mercy extended to us. Someone brought us understanding and we had a revelation of our own lack resulting in our discovery of our own Need of Him. We lay aside our own self-sufficiency and choose His truth over our own, we choose a dependent posture upon Him and His work and word to save us like a child upon a parent, this is abiding in the vine. The Holy Spirit leads and teaches us into all truth. Over these years since 1981 and my first surrender to God I look back and see much error in my life that God has corrected me, some very painful and in my wake, some wreckage, I inadvertently hurt people. I consider and hope over time people get less ignorant when your heart is for the truth and the word of God is found in us. The Spirit builds in us block upon block, faith upon faith ever-growing in better understanding and dependence upon Jesus Himself this is a never ending deal. Here is an example. **Romans 1:17.**

A brother in Christ I knew was struggling financially it was harming him and his family and I addressed it in my private time with the Lord in Prayer. I could see it in his wife eyes she was hurting because of His foolish behavior. I had the means to aid him but the Lord would not allow me to help him or his family. When I spoke to the individual, I always pointed him to Christ for him to seek out his answers from Jesus himself, but it seemed to me that his prayer life was deficient he wanted to do it his own way. Over the years, the Lord never allowed me to aid him while I loved them both but God never revealed why, not my business I suppose. The Lord taught me something, that sometimes Jesus is working on someone and when we come in and bail them out or rescue them, we have hindered the work of the Lord in them. My heart was to renew and help my friend but I sought out the spirits Guidance the spirit to guide me while I was desiring to be loving, giving and kind to someone. This is an example of abiding in Him, allowing Jesus to overrule your desire to be kind and loving which is good to someone, in favor of being obedient to God and His purposes.

I suppose this is why Jesus says, "I do as the Father bids me to do" and "I do nothing of Myself but as the father taught me." So, this situation stayed in prayer for years as they struggled. I would not stop loving folks because I was overly caucus. It is always better to error on the side of love when in doubt of what to do. But I practiced looking away unto Jesus the author and finisher of my faith and He said STOP, in this case He was working on Him.

But now I realize I was there not to bail him out of his pains but to point Him to his answer, Jesus. That was the ultimate love the 100-fold answer to love to Give my friend Jesus, to be my friends sign post pointing him to Jesus Himself to be the answer in my friend's heart and struggle. **1 Thessalonians 4:1.**

As a Man Thinks in His Heart So is He

Change the Way I think, O Lord

Acts 2:38 (AMP)

38 And Peter said to them, "<u>Repent [change your old way of thinking</u>, turn from your sinful ways, accept and follow Jesus as the Messiah] and be baptized, each of you, in the name of Jesus Christ because of the forgiveness of your sins; and you will receive the gift of the Holy Spirit.

Repentance is a change of the way you think. Thinking and acting like Jesus, His ways over rules my own ways. Read **Isaiah 55:8-9** If I think like Christ then I will act like Christ because as a man thinks so is he. **Proverbs 23:7a** Somehow, we have been taught that repentance is saying I am sorry to God. He already knows your sorry, miserable, pour and deceived. He is and was always about heart change that results in Godly thinking thus in doing. For as a man thinks in his heart so is he in his actions and doings. Change your thinking.

It is:
- Deny yourself and take up your cross and follow Him, laying down your right to be right but to choose His way over your own ways. **Matthew 16:24.**
- I can do all things through Christ who strengthens me. **Philippians 4:13.**
- Abide in the vine for without Him you can do no-thing. **John 15:5.**

- It is the abandonment of my own ways and thinking and living and doing His ways of thinking and living. **Isaiah 55:8-9.**
- Walk in Love, walk in the light **Ephesians 5:2,8.**
- He who says he abides in Him, ought himself also walk just as He walked, looking away unto His source as we do the same.**1 John 2:6.**
- Let us walk in the same pattern, let us be of the same mind. On my own I can do no-thing. But with Him I can do all things. **Philippians 3:16-17.**
- Allow God's love to train you in Godly thinking even if it hurts a bit. **Hebrews 12:11.**
- Walk worthy, walk in Him, walk in wisdom walk even as he walked in submission and in a dependent posture even like a child to his parent. **Colossians 1:10, 2:6, 4:5.**
- For as a man thinks in his heart so is he in his actions **Proverbs 23:7a.**

How to Deal With Sinning Brothers

Matthew 18:15-17 Jesus Speaking (NKJV)

"Moreover if your brother sins against you, go and tell him his fault between you and him alone. If he hears you, you have gained your brother. [16] But if he will not hear, take with you one or two more, that 'by the mouth of two or three witnesses every word may be established.' [17] And if he refuses to hear them, tell it to the church. But if he refuses even to hear the church, let him be to you like a heathen and a tax collector."

Jesus gives the wisdom of how to deal with error or sin you come in contact within others. This verse reveals you go to them one on one, like a friend would, face to face. Error abounds in the church today; I say this with sorrow in my heart. Gossip, trashing, and bashing is in the church, But the word says offence and being offended will come in the last days but I hope not from your mouth. Even Jesus says, "woe unto them that bring offences." **Matthew 18:7 (NKJV)**

Jude 1:18 (AMP)

18 They used to say to you, "In the last days there will be scoffers, following after their own ungodly passions."

These are folks following their own ways. Scoffers, opinionated, haters, and trollers on the internet and in the churches are being revealed, even today. I will forgive them, God can forgive them, and I hope all of these misguided ones today that bring offence would find repentance inside and outside of the church. Some very large churches and pastors have revealed their own shame and begun to take shots at other Christ followers publicly. This brings shame to the Lord because you will not exercise your wisdom from the word of **Matthew 18:15-17** and pray for the deception in your brother or neighbor's way. Preferring rather bring and sow condemning divisive words that you will soon reap. You have sat in a chair you do not belong. Even worse, you have taught others to do the same. Choose rather overlook and care for the sins of your brothers. Or address it humbly one on one with kindness and love in your heart, this should always be the path for the Christ follower. Draw close to them to create change in them if able, otherwise if you don't care to make the effort, then keep your mouth shut and sin not. Keep your eyes and mind on the Lord and not in your brother's backyard looking at his junk, lack, and errors when you have your own junk, lack, and errors to deal with. **Isaiah 26:3.**

Jesus did not come to condemn the world at this time read **John 3:17** or its contents, neither should you? For they belong to Him and they are for Him alone to straighten out and Judge later, they will answer to Him and so will you. Every knee shall bow and give account for every word, think on this. **Matthew 12:36** You have jumped into a seat you do not belong when you become the opinionated critic eating from the tree of good and evil, this is Satan's bait to SIN. Think on it! The accuser of the brethren's work, you are doing for him with your mouth.

2 Peter 3:3 (AMP)

3 First of all, know [without any doubt] that mockers will come in the last days with their mocking, following after their own human desires…

It grieves my heart to say that both of the above scriptures are happening today scoffers, mockers, dividers, and jealousy, within the church, it is to our shame and the Lord's shame, but outside the church it is expected. My heart breaks because we are so willing to ignorantly judge our brothers in this world. God said to LOVE and pick up your cross, what happened? We have strayed from His path and left His word behind and now we will soon reap what we have sown. We stay contented with salvation in the outer court and doing as we think is good and never entered the inner court were we lay down our own ways to pick up His ways.

Galatians 5:22-25 (NKJV)

22 But the fruit of the Spirit is love, joy, peace, longsuffering, kindness, goodness, faithfulness, 23 gentleness, self-control. Against such there is no law. 24 And those who are Christ's have crucified the flesh with its passions and desires. 25 If we live in the Spirit, let us also walk in the Spirit. 26 Let us not become conceited, provoking one another, envying one another.

This is inner court thinking… discipleship thinking, bearing fruit thinking V24 says we have crucified the flesh with its self-nature passions but we have not today. Remember "i" is the letter, in the middle of sin. V22-26 I could stop here and be done with the lesson but the word says, "out of the mouths of two or three let everything be established" **Deuteronomy 19:15** So I will provide more than plenty of verses to nail this concept down and lock the door that Gossip and speaking destructively, disparagingly out of one's mouth about anyone and I mean anyone is SIN and it brings shame to Christ because you say you follow Him. But your mouth proves you follow another, the accuser.

Proverbs 6:16-20 (AMP)

16 These six things the Lord hates; Indeed, seven are repulsive to Him:

17 A proud look [the attitude that makes one overestimate oneself and discount others, a lying tongue and hands that shed innocent blood,

18 A heart that creates wicked plans, Feet that run swiftly to evil,

19 A false witness who breathes out lies [even half-truths], And one who spreads discord (disagreeable rumors) among brothers.

Well, if God hates it, I will not do it, God help me! V17a.19b I have to remind myself that God uses imperfect vessels to do a portion of His perfect work, get this and understand it, this is vital no one is perfect. None of us has it all figured out, we know in part. **1 Corinthians 13:9** None of us is without sin. We need Christ and each other. Jesus deliberately worked it out that way so we could not be an island unto ourselves. Forcing us to learn to love and need one another because we are one body in Christ. The message to the church today is Learn to LOVE one another now press in and work it out. Help me love my brothers Lord, without you I will fail but with you I can do all things. I trust and rely on you to keep my mouth and mind clear of being the critic of my brother and working for the accuser.

Romans 16:17-20 (NKJV) "Avoid Divisive People"

17 Now I urge you, brethren, note those who cause divisions and offenses, contrary to the doctrine which you learned, and avoid them. 18 For those who are such do not serve our Lord Jesus Christ, but their own belly, and by smooth words and flattering speech deceive the hearts of the simple. 19 For your obedience has become known to all. Therefore, I am glad on your behalf; but I want you to be wise in what is good, and simple concerning evil. 20 And the God of peace will crush Satan under your feet shortly.

Be careful, many push others down to elevate themselves, but love overlooks a fault or a deficient character trait of another brother or sister. Yet they will not allow LOVE to have its perfect work in us, the work of the cross. Jesus is my hiding place and my answer. I will sow mercy and grace in others so that I may reap the same from others and God. This is how we ought to think and live in Christ. **John 3:17.** Those that judge, divide over opinions, even correct doctrinal ones, having an internal desire and a secret wanting to be right or above his brother. **Romans 12:16** But to win with God is to lose in our self-nature, your own rightness. [Sarx in Greek] **Romans 8:6**. Pick up your cross deny your self-nature the "i" in you and follow Jesus, Saints. Let Jesus be your victory and hide in Him. **Psalms 91** This is you and I yielding, surrendering, it is the bride's full submission to the groom that He desires from me and you the bride. He will defend His bride let Him.

Ponder this statement very carefully; You do not have the right to be right and set yourself above another? But you only have the right to be the fulfilment of grace and mercy and the servant of them all and be broken bread and pour out wine for Jesus and His use. **Mark 9:35.**

Did Jesus wash your feet? Did Jesus take the nails in His hands and feet for you? Did Jesus, while you were a sinner, come near to befriend you and revealed to you, the need to abandon yourself and choose Him to be your Savior? He drew close while you were sinning.

V19 Be wise in what is good, be a student and study Jesus via His word and do not focus on evil Saints at all, for it will reveal its own ugly head, do not seek to look for it in others. Know what is Good and the opposite shall expose itself. Study God for He is Good and His ways are Good and you will know what is divergent. Keep your Mind and your eyes stayed on Him for He will Keep you in perfect peace. Stop comparing yourself to others and being the critic with your tongue and mouth.

Listen to this......The doctrine of division, is like a veiled shadow of hate, darkness, wickedness posturing as light and

wisdom Even Satan temped Eve with words that looked wise and it is happening today in the Church. I have heard pastors take shots at denominations this and is not the way of the Lord. Critics act, influenced by Satan eating from the tree of good and evil and the accuser influences lives there. You will know them by their fruit and how they act. Where did this fruit come from the tree of Life or the tree of good and evil. For as a man thinks in his heart, so is he in his actions.

Galatians 5:14 (AMP)

14 For the whole Law [concerning human relationships] is fulfilled in one precept, "You shall love your neighbor as yourself [that is, you shall have an unselfish concern for others and do things for their benefit]."

Again, God reveals the concept of sowing and reaping even in this verse with the command to love and over look.

This is the determination of this message, the exposure of lack of effectiveness of the Christ following church today is because we will not do the work of growing up into Christ and exhibiting His love for one another as He commanded us. We are happy with what God has done for us: salvation and baptism, the outer court, but we deny our Lord what we should do for Him in the inner court, here lives discipleship and sanctification the picking up of the cross in you. We deny the work of the cross in us then we fail Him whom we say we follow. Look when it comes to salvation and the work of Jesus and the Cross it is all done, nothing can be added, it is finished gloriously and permanently. But when it comes to discipleship, the cross has just begun to work in you and me. Many churches have focused on the teaching the outer court and stop at the cross of Christ and salvation and baptism; this is the outer court of the Temple of God. But the inner court is all about discipleship, knowing Him thus understanding the standard to be like Him. A hearing ear is developed and the willingness to obey, incense for prayer and meditation, menorah candles of wisdom and the study of the shewbread, the Word of God, Jesus Himself. Study and eat whom you want to be like, there is no way around this. Jesus is the tree of life, eat from His fruit. Satan is in the deception of good he appeals to the "i" in you, resist him with the word of truth and he shall flee.

We go back to **Psalms 1 and 119** Study Jesus's ways, thinking and pondering His reactions and actions in the inner court. Emulation of Jesus in us is our goal. To be a carbon copy, a direct duplicate, of Him is my goal. Meditation of His word and principles living in our hearts so we can do as He does. Being redeemers of this world is our work, but vitally united in a dependent posture upon HIM like a child unto a parent Jesus our Lord is the only way and our only source. Look at a picture of the temple of Solomon and ponder this a moment. Preaching the outer court alone is good but not the whole gospel, it is not the end. But the door to discipleship opens on the other side of the cross and His kingdom coming down in you on earth as it is in heaven, but this happens after you enter this second door, the inner court. If you do not understand this or God has not revealed this to you yet, put it on a shelf for later consumption. Please don't throw this truth away do not poo-poo this. Read **1 Peter 2:5-9**, NKJV.

- **The outer court:** The alter is where the lamb was Sacrifice Jesus died for our sins and the laver is for washing is symbolic of our baptism and new life we have in Jesus Christ. [What He has done for us is 100 % done and finished perfectly and permanently for no one can take me from His hand]
- **The inner court:** is where learning about His Holiness and doing occurs. Incense for prayer and meditation life in you becomes alive this is without fail the most lacking in the church, **Psalms 1 and 119** The menorah candle is for wisdom and understanding is growing in you and

the study of shewbread for the word of God living in you alive, this is where your relationship with Christ and the word thrives and lives and becomes alive and powerful. Here we follow, listen, and obey Christ and pick up our cross and follow His ways of doing and thinking. This is what we do for Him as a response to His love and mercy, the gift He gave us in the outer court. He gave me His life; I give Him mine.

- **Holy of Holies:** Then there is a Holy of Holies. Only the High Priest enters here. This is where we/you become kings and priest like Him. **Hebrews 6:20** Jesus being the first of the order of Melchizedek meaning King Priest. Read **Revelation 1:6** This is where you lay down your life for church as an intercessor praying, declaring, and decreeing the will of the Father over His kingdom. Here is no greater love than to lay down one's life down for His friends in the church and the world in intersession. What does the High Priest do in the Holy of Holies? He sprinkles blood on the alter for his people's redemption, salvation, revelation of truth. What do we do? The same, pray for the redemption and revealing of the truth in the church and praying for the people of God and those He has given you. Everyone should have a Priestly role for one's own children then extend your love to the world and pray for their salvation in to truth. **I Peter 2:1-2,4-5.**

Listen to this…The church at large is interested in what God has done for them, the outer court grace and mercy but the inner court is what you will do for Him from the abundance of your love and relationship to Him. i.e., good works without a dependent, reliant relationship is worthless work according to the word of **Matthew 25:12**. Telling people to serve in the church without them having a relationship with Jesus Himself and the word is a set up for them to fail. I have had pastors get so upset at me for this statement. Pick up your cross and be set apart for His use from the abundance of your relationship to Him then and only then serve Him from there. Jesus said love God first then love His people. **Matthew 10:37** In our Churches we need the first commandment, to LOVE GOD taught and modeled by our pastors and leadership. What that looks like and how to do it? It is explained here in this book. God wants the first of everything. First of your time in prayer and study, money, I say this and some stumble over it. There are churches today that are not very good at modeling the love for the Word, meditation, and the prayer life of the inner court. Some are very happy preaching the outer court, salvation and baptism alone.

Never do good works absent from a relationship and dependent posture with Him, this leads to error and burn out. Read **Matthew 7:21-23**, **Matthew 25:12** Remember you are the temple of God and God has shown you what His temple and His people look like **1 Corinthians 6:19**. Jesus lived and thrived in the living of the three rooms of the temple of God we ought to do the same. Ponder this a bit.

Luke 9:23 (NKJV)

Then He said to them all, "If anyone desires to come after Me, let him deny himself, and take up his cross daily, and follow Me."

Why did Jesus say "if anyone desires to come after me?" Because He is our creator and He understands when we see people we admire we want to do as they do to be as they are. Look at our kids admiring their sport heroes. Emulation is the next step for them. So Christ knew some wanted to be like Him then the next step to emulation and duplication is leaving the outer court and come into inner court where discipline and cross where we get the word discipleship from. Here is the work of the cross working in you. Go in to all the world and make disciples this is the effort of this ministry **Luke 9:23, Matthew 16:24,28:19 Mark 8:34, 1 Corinthians 6:19.**

Truth Is in Our Dependence

Matthew 7:21-23 (NKJV)

Not everyone who says to Me, 'Lord, Lord,' shall enter the kingdom of heaven, but he who does the will of My Father in heaven. ²² Many will say to Me in that day, 'Lord, Lord, have we not prophesied in Your name, cast out demons in Your name, and done many wonders in Your name?' ²³ And then I will declare to them, 'I never knew you; depart from Me, you who practice lawlessness!'

"Hey Lord, I was an usher, I was a leader of this and that, I worked in the food court, coffee cart, worship team." Then Jesus replies, "depart from me you **independent** workers without reliance dependence or relationship upon me." The word lawless in Greek is the word for independent without relationship with me. Without vital connection like a water hose disconnected from the spigot its source. Doing and serving absent from relationship to Me. For without Me you can do no-thing of eternal value Jesus Says. You do not abide in the vine. You have no relationship with Me and My word. Depart from me Jesus says….. woe you might say. I say it as well you must LOVE GOD FIRST and His word and pray and meditate on Him and His ways before you become a servant in the church. What? Boy, I know, I stepped in it big time, so what, I have ticked off so many pastors big time and later those same pastors come back to me to say I was right. But it is not about being right, but we know in part and we need one another to get the full picture of who Jesus is and we are to become like Him. Here in this reading is my part to give to the Church.

Relationship: It is error to teach from the pulpit "serve your church or community" absent from the servant's relationship to Jesus Christ himself our source via prayer and meditation life working in them. Sorry, it is what it is. Meaning a prayer/meditation/study life on Christ and a dependent posture of needing Him in all that I do, for without Him I cannot do NO-thing. A dependent posture is required. Not independence here. Even Jesus had a dependent posture upon His Father in **John 5:30** and if He did, how much more should we? If Jesus modeled it, we should walk even as he walked and model it as well. Read these Verses. **John 5:30, 15:1-6, Philippians 4:13** these verses reveal dependency like a child upon a parent we should need our new Parent, our source Jesus Himself via the Spirit. With Christ as your centered relationship in prayer times you can serve but absent of it you are in danger. read **Matthew 7:21-23, 25:12 and 18:2-6.**

Lawless one: The word lawless in verse 23 means "independent one" in the Greek. So doing church works absent of me says Jesus, abiding in the vine, not having a relationship with Jesus makes me lawless and independent of Him and this is error. The world does charity work but absent of relationship and it will have no eternal value. Here is the safe way to address this issue…. my service is always from the abundance of my relationship to and with Him, I must know Him, love Him, and He must know me. My purpose is to fill myself with Him, love God, first eating from the tree of Life. I eat from the tree and fill my cup and my cup with God is full and over flowing and then give Him away to the world the cup runs over to touch and fill others it gives them a taste of Him. The river of living waters is from the source Jesus and that is the drink that quenches and changes the hearts of Men. If I give away myself, it bears no good fruit. But sow good seed in good ground, I sow Jesus in someone's heart it will bare everlasting seed and fruit forever. Before you dump on this concept, or take offense, read on a bit.

Example of the independent one: Over twenty years ago I addressed this very issue with three pastors of a church of 2,000 folks I was attending. I was also a Bible study teacher at my home as a part of this church. I casually knew the pastors and they knew me. I saw an older team leader, an acquaintance of mine serving in the church for over five years, walking down the steps of the church and he had a long face. I had concern for him and I asked him how he was doing and he advised me of his troubles with his ministry at the church. It seemed to me that he needed direction from God to help him, as we all do, so I asked him. "How is your prayer life going?" and he replied, "WHAT WAS THAT?" Inside, I was so angered I wanted to vomit. I was hurting that this servant had never had a relationship with Our Lord Jesus these five years of his ministry time at this church. He was serving from and empty cup. His efforts were of no Godly value. His source was himself. He was doing Matthew 7:22. This poor guy was serving from himself for five years and nobody cared to teach him a prayer life of dependency upon Christ. He was stuck in the outer court serving and never knew there was more to God. He had fire insurance but no relationship. So, I called a meeting with the pastors and myself alone to address this issue.

I explained what had occurred I could see that some of the leaders were ashamed then some became offended and defensive during the discussion. One of the three pastors agreed with me and said that they could do better job teaching the love for the word of God, prayer, and dependent posture upon Christ in the church especially for anyone serving. This church was very much an outer court church meaning they taught salvation, baptism, and community service and that was the end of that. It was not very well received as it was a reflection of the leadership's lack of teaching of prayer and intimacy with Christ the inner court concepts. Now looking back, prayer and intimacy with Christ must be the core of all servant's life even pastor's life in the church with all teams including worship teams. Jesus says my house will be a house of prayer and we do not teach that we are His house and temple and that we all need a prayer life. Because without Him I cannot do nothing, but with Him, I can do all things. Do you get it now? Do you see where I am going? Even if you read this objectively you will have to agree that the error was the lack of Psalms 1 and 119:9-16 working in this individual servant's life.

He was serving and only had the outer court experience of salvation. But we are the temple, the house of God a house of prayer. **I Peter 2:5** Jesus calls us living stones to that temple that has three rooms. **1 Corinthians 1:16,17,19** The egg cannot produce with the yoke only or any of the three parts missing. It needs all three sections, shell, egg white and yoke to be of any good reproductive use, so it is with us. This is how we love God first; this is how we do Psalms 1 and 119:9-16 by allowing the temple concept to work and take root in us and in the church. This is how we live and teach the kingdom. We must, after the outer court of salvation and baptism enter the inner court of discipleship and sanctification here is our relationship with God developed. Here is where we know Him and He know us. This is how you avoid **Matthew 7:22-23** happening to you. After being saved we must enter into discipleship it is different than and more than salvation experience. Look up "Hebrew temple of God" or Google "Soloman's temple 3d" you can see a nice video.

Think about the unity of the church you would have if everyone in the body has a prayer life with Jesus, a study of Jesus life, a dependent posture upon the vine Jesus Christ life. Jesus is the tree of life. We, the church, need to feed on Him, all of creation groans for this.

As a Man Thinks in His Heart So is He

LOVE YOUR BROTHERS

I Corinthians 12:12 (NKJV)

12 For as the body is one and has many members, but all the members of that one body, being many, are one body, so also is Christ.

The curious thing here is that **Chapter 12 of Corinthians** it speaks of the oneness of the body of Christ that Jesus our King desires for us and we should live by and the very next Chapter **13 "Love Chapter"** tells us the church **how to** do it. How to become the Church and bride of Christ? Today, we do not overlook sin of our brothers but we blast them on the internet for many to see our own shame and dishonor. We will not address it one on one because we are cowards. We ourselves have not entered the inner court or the Most Holy place of knowing HIM.

This was no accident that these chapters 12 and 13 are so displayed in the Bible. Just like **Psalms 1** it is intentional in its location and priority. Do you think that the Jew and Greek in Jesus day Worshiped God in the same approach, method or manner? I cannot prove it, but I think it was vastly different and the one church could have been offended by the other churches methods. Do you think they had different peripheral doctrines, expressions and beliefs? Are those reasons to divide oneself from another? You can choose to not participate with something disagreeable or unbiblical. But you must embrace the Christ in them.

I Corinthians 12:13-21 (NKJV)

For by one Spirit we were all baptized into one body— whether Jews or Greeks, whether slaves or free—and have all been made to drink into one Spirit. 14 For in fact the body is not one member but many.

15 If the foot should say, "Because I am not a hand, I am not of the body," is it therefore not of the body? 16 And if the ear should say, "Because I am not an eye, I am not of the body," is it therefore not of the body? 17 If the whole body were an eye, where would be the hearing? If the whole were hearing, where would be the smelling? 18 But now God has set the members, each one of them, in the body just as He pleased. 19 And if they were all one member, where would the body be? 20 But now indeed there are many members, yet one body. 21 And the eye cannot say to the hand, "I have no need of you"; nor again the head to the feet, "I have no need of you."

Do you think He is talking to you about your congregation only or do you think He is talking about the church that calls itself after His name worldwide? We are one body in Christ and none of us can say, "I do not need you" to another because they are different, maybe different Ministry emphasis or style. We are one in Christ! v25 We lack in maturity in Christ when we divide ourselves from our Brothers IN CHRIST because we think we are right or righter and our ways are right in our own eyes. But you cannot live without a stomach. My brothers, please humbly consider these words and change the way you think. I must admit I am writing this because I think there is a better way. I must be thinking I am right, in my own eyes but we should use the Word of God to validate a concept of thinking and not for the destruction of a person or Ministry of another, ever. Be a builder, and restorer in His kingdom work, learn to love now. Stay out of the Spiritual demolition business this belong to the Spirit of God. If we truly build the kingdom of God, we automatically dismantle the kingdom of darkness no need to focus on what's not right in others but build what is right in Gods eyes in yourself then in others. Learn to see others even if they lack understanding learn to see them like God sees them. Be willing to keep your mouth shut for their sake. They may not be ready to receive revelation you have yet. Even Jesus said in **John 6:12 "Oh, there is so much more I want to tell you, but you can't understand it now.**

John 13:35, NKJV. Jesus Speaking

"By this, all will know that you are My disciples, if you have love for one another."

You and I cannot escape this? Jesus is saying you MUST Love. And love overlooks a fault or error in your brother and neighbor or another ministry and holds no ill towards your enemies but prays for them and maybe lovingly corrects them one on one someday. Did not the Lord Himself love Abraham and Sarah full of errors, sin of lying, disobedient in doubt? God used them despite their errors and loved them. He later called Abraham the father of Faith even when he was faithless? When we are in Christ, we must stop dividing over whatever differences we have with one others ministries or denominations. It is not our place to judge the servant of Our Master even if we do not agree with their methods of ministry in any way. They serve God and not you. Love for one another is care and kindness smothered in grace and mercy for one another. How is slamming, verbally abusing another being a Christ Follower? Smashing and bashing on the internet or privately how is it reflective or resembling our Lord Christ? I can't get there. Slamming someone on the internet or in emails is more like the accuser of the brethren's work. Think on this....

If you say you love them and want to correct them why not become their friend and win them over to your thinking? These are Godly steps revealed by Christ. Some have said to me, "They follow another Jesus or a false Jesus" as a motive to be a critic of another people group. I think I would approach things differently. First, only Christ can judge the hearts of men this is far above my office to judge. I will not judge, but I will love, draw, and show kindness so I can salt and re-salt them when I can. This way I sow and reap LOVE and Kindness and not judgment in my life. **Galatians 6:7, Romans 12:10, Romans 13:8, Isaiah 54:17, John 3:17.**

There are ministries I disagree with doctrinally, no doubt, but my choice is to aid them in seeing the truth via one on one or shut my mouth outwardly and inwardly pray for their illumination of understanding for the truth and that is the end of it. This can be a Holy of Holies priestly effort in me to intercede for them in love.

But it is never okay to gossip, troll, or express outwardly a disparaging comment which is divisive, destructive, and unloving. But I can teach what I think is right even if it goes against the grain of the aforementioned ministry but I do caution you never to use ministers or ministry names or any identifiable in your arguments. The point is to teach the truth and not to point out others errors unless we are one on one with them. The Lord says, "Get wisdom and in your getting get understanding." Therefore, I teach understanding of the truth in Love. It is useless to tell someone get saved! Unless you tell them how to get save. That is this attempt in this to book to give you the How-To's. **God is more interested in you loving your brother even with errors in their life than you being right about a topic or thing.** Think on this? learn to love, learn to overlook but always pointing them to the word of truth and Christ! I can be right about a topic with my wife but I lost and broke the relationship because I wanted to be right more than to learn to love her and draw her to the truth in love. Do you see the difference? Have you seen it in your own life? You have lost the war because you wanted to win the battle. You lose being right and hurting your wife, the gift God has given you. It is better to wait until she is ready for the truth. Gently bring her along in the washing word and prayer, it will wash and renew her thinking unto Holiness Jesus Goal for everyone.

Colossians 3:12 (AMP)

12 So, as God's own chosen people, who are holy [set apart, sanctified for His purpose] and well-beloved [by God Himself], put on a heart of compassion, kindness, humility, gentleness, and patience [which has the power to endure whatever injustice or unpleasantness comes, with good temper];

Read **Colossians 3:12 AMP** above, read it again and again, think on it a bit.

It is work, to have the cross working in us, it is heavy to choose **love over rightness**. It takes effort to paddle against the stream and not flow with the current, the easy way. It is not passive to follow Christ while carrying your cross to follow Him. We take the kingdom by force by willingly yielding to God's ways of thinking. But you cannot know Gods ways without you being a student and studying His word. **Luke 9:23 (AMP)**

How did Jesus walk? Jesus is our model pattern SON and He Overlooked your SIN and the sin of others so that He may win you over to His side by forgiveness and the gift of grace. He overlooks your error. Learn to hate sin but love the sinner just as Jesus did. Will we follow and do the same for others as He has done for us? Jesus did this for the disciples, did He not? Jesus did it for the crowds that came to Him, did He not? He over looked errors and sin in others until they had a ready heart to receive correction and change of mind that equals repentance. He taught Holiness high and lifted up knowing it was too high for the sinner to reach on their own but the very Holiness He preached revealed our need for Him to help us for without Him we can do no-thing. To learn to abide in the vine, because with Him I can do all things…

Once you truly know Christ and Holy Spirit works in you and changing your heart and mind, this is the process of sanctification, discipleship, and repentance gloriously working in you going forward this is a daily event. This is the inner court of the temple and you have become the bride that is ready for Her groom to come and get her. You have established a solid relationship with Jesus, your groom. You have started to prepare your garments for Him. The work of a yielded heart that says, "yes" to Him our Master, Our Lord King, Jesus, vs your own rights and rightness. You have submitted to your groom your husband you have chosen His ways over your own ways. It is the Yes, you say to the Spirit, cautious not to grieve Him while you are in the way, yearning to have perked up ears to hear Him and obey. When He tells you to love the unlovely, do it, shut your mouth and do it. **Read Romans 12** Our lives are no longer our own, it belongs to Him, He paid for it with His blood, that's the deal you accept Christ and you belong to Him and you must live His way and not your own way for ever more. Read **1 Corinthians 6:20** These ninety years of life do not compare to eternity with Him. The mind of Christ can be ours today but we need to be wholly His. First submit to your husband O bride. We all are His bride some prepare to glory for our groom, He will soon come and fetch us. Blessed is He for He is HOLY and we are His bride, follow Him and live dependent upon Him, love Him, study Him because He first loved us.

Repentance is not a one-time deal my friends; it is a daily event where I say, "Not my way but your way, O my Lord." **Isaiah 55:8-9** Repentance is the ever changing of thinking to His ways of thinking and so doing. **Romans 12:2** It is the picking up of the cross, it is the sanctifying cleansing of the bride working in me and you. It is me obeying My FATHER that said obey and follow, My Son, Jesus cleanse your garments O Bride, It is your yes Lord, allowing the working of the Spirit of God in You, as you yield to His hand and His voice. Be the overcomer by yielding to the groom our master Jesus, Our Lord and King. **Revelation 3:5**

It is the filling of your lamp oil being prepared for our Grooms arrival with His word of truth waiting and alive for His Presence to arrive to your circumstances of earthly brokenness and readiness for His presences.

We are His bride and for some reason the bride wants her own ways. But the groom gives you options and says if you want to live in my kingdom now on earth, you will have to learn to yield to Me, submit to Me, says Christ. I am the author and the finisher of your faith says Jesus, trust and reliance must be in me says the Lord. The answer is hidden in Me says Jesus. For the Groom is the King and Lord master of His kingdom, Jesus Christ our Lord. **Isaiah 62:5, Matthew 9:15,** His throne is His alone and we live and thrive in our submission to Him but we fight for our own rights disrupting corrupting our own peace and the church suffers for it. Our own ways reveal the lack of the cross working in us frustrating the work of the King and His kingdom. Your yielded submission, O bride, is required, for the Groom's seed to bare Holy and Glorious Fruit of Holy everlasting increase, it is in your waiting, yielding, and overcoming of your self-nature, your sinful "i" in you.

As a Man Thinks in His Heart So is He

The Stone

Matthew 21:44 (NKJV)

"And whoever falls on this stone will be broken; but on whomever it falls, it will grind him to powder."

The Spirit says to me "fall upon the Stone," I interpret this to mean choose to *humble yourself* before Him, submit yourself to the groom, O bride, or the stone will fall upon you and grind you to powder until you find humility. The idea here is you choose how God presents Himself in these years of life He has given you, as an alter to redemption and change to be like Him or Jesus allowing life's grinding stone driving you to the alter of humility and submission.

I Peter 2:4-9

You will arrive to humility one way or another. This is why every knee shall bow before Him. But God advises Humble yourself, **James 4:10 AMP** or He will allow the stone of life to humble you. No one escapes His hand, no one will be able to say "I did not know." "He disciplines the ones He loves" and "He so loved the world," do you see it? No one escapes, He loves the people of the world- His children. You can choose to fall on your knees before Him **James 4:10 AMP, I Peter 5:5-9** or have Him allow life to drive you to your knees until humility and willing submission is found in you. I hear God saying, "Pick one."

Wake up, Saints!

Compare the Hebrew Temple of God to Israel in Exodus and to your own life. You can go around the mountain for forty years for a trip that should have only taken eleven days to cross by foot from Egypt through the wilderness to the promised land of Israel. It was the Nation of Israel's lack of humility and dependence upon God that kept them ever learning and never coming to the understanding of God's love for them. It was a heart problem for them and for us this whole thing is repeating in the church today, can you see it? **2 Timothy 3:7** Did you know Egypt means "darkness?" He brought you out of darkness of this world into Salvation His marvelous light and you are making your way through this life in the wilderness until the promised land appears!

This is the outer court, He brought them out of the land of Egypt He brought you into salvation the outer court. Both Israel, and Christians, were taken out of the land of darkness and sin. Many came into the wilderness but few went into the promise land do you want to be the one that makes that same mistake as Israel did? Trust and rely in God, abandon yourself and humbly learn from your lessons, hate sin and grow up into Christ and become the brother of Christ He intended you to be. Let the temple pattern have its work completed in you. **Romans 8:29** Cleanse your garment O bride **Revelation 16:15** with the fruits righteousness of your changed ways of thinking which is repentance. "For as a man thinks in his heart, so is he" in his actions. Do not have the evil heart of unbelief like in **Hebrews 3:12,** this is a dangerous place to be stuck in. It is a sign from the Lord that He wants me to see something but I am not getting it. I have asked the Lord to aid me in getting rid of my "stinken thinken" when I feel the lessons are repeating over and over.

Matthew 5:3 (AMP)

3 "Blessed [spiritually prosperous, happy, to be admired] are the poor in spirit [those devoid of spiritual arrogance, those who regard themselves as

insignificant], for theirs is the kingdom of heaven [both now and forever].

It seems to me that the kingdom of heaven can be ours now in this life and we do not need to wait for death or rapture to obtain this Kingdom life being alive in us today. Living in the kingdom is living in the Promised Land here and now. Do you believe this that the kingdom of God is in you? **Luke 17:21** this verse in Luke says it is. It would be cruel if Jesus gave us the Beatitudes and said you get these rewards only when you die and go to heaven. What would be the point to that? He is looking for some to enter the kingdom of promise here and now the whole of creation is groaning until now. To walk even as He walked to Live even as He lived to do even as He did. Read **Mark 16:14, Romans 11:23, Hebrews 3:12,19.**

Hebrews 3:18-19 (NKJV)

18 And to whom did He swear that they would not enter His rest, but to those who did not obey? 19 So we see that they could not enter in because of unbelief.

Listen to this, we ought to regard ourselves as nothing- a zero with the rim rubbed out. We are His and for His use. Humble people are refreshing folks, have you ever noticed? Teachableness is the meaning for meekness in Greek. It is a key to growth with God it is the stance that "I know nothing as I ought," it is the marker of humility and awareness that I need Him or I am lost. You fully understand, you are nothing without Him. But with Him, you can do all things. **Philippians 4:13.**

_____

_____

_____

_____

_____

_____

_____

_____

_____

_____

_____

_____

_____

_____

_____

_____

_____

_____

_____

_____

_____

_____

_____

_____

As a Man Thinks in His Heart So is He

SERVANTS SERVING THE CHURCH

Provers 18:11 (AMP)

Good sense and discretion make a man slow to anger, And it is his honor and glory to overlook a transgression or an offense [without seeking revenge and harboring resentment].

You do not have the right to be RIGHT to set yourself above another, you only have the right to be broken, broken bread, and poured out wine for His use, to be the greatest of these is to be the servant of them all. **Mark 9:35** Because He modeled this for us when He went to the cross. He sought out what was best for another and not for Himself while suffering for it. He foresaw the Glory of redemption of humanity before Him. Are we followers of Jesus, we are to walk even as He walked? Seek out the lower spot saints? Read **Mark 9:35, John 10:27, 1 John 2:6.**

Jesus, over and over, is willing to forgive your faults and errors, and loves you so that He may draw you close, so that you may know Him better to salt and re-salt to prune and re-prune, to seed and re-seed to water and re-water. Do you do the same for others when they stink with sin, my friends? Jesus gave you grace and mercy while you were in rebellion as an enemy of the kingdom, we should give it to others as well? We are to walk even as He walked being a reconciler to the world, peacemaker between God and Man and man and man. **1 John 2:6** We should be restorers, rebuilders, healers of humankind and not destructive or critical to man and his weaknesses to sin. **2 Corinthians 5:18.**

Jesus came to provide a method for forgiveness and the restoration to what was broken to all generation that may come after Him, we ought to do the same. Jesus Loved the man that hammered the nails into His hands and feet, that spat on Him, that said blessed are you that comes in the name… and later proclaimed crucify Him. Love over comes, Love never fails, love overlooks the weakness to sin of another, will you do the same? **1 Corinthians 16:14.**

This does not mean we compromise the truth or weaken the truth from the pulpit or otherwise because of love you can HATE sin and the brokenness it brings but you must LOVE the sinner. But it may mean that I have patience with an individual until they can with understanding and accept the whole truth of God fully. I had many friends that struggled and I admonished them to learn to Hate SIN just as God does. If you see a weakness in yourself that you know God does not approve of, learn to hate it, you will soon stop doing it soon enough. It works with anything porn, drinking, smoking, cursing, whatever sin it may be talk to it and say over and over, "I hate you" and mean it in your heart, soon you will stop doing it, learn to hate sin. **Proverbs 8:13**.

I can go on with this concept or principle and it would take days. Picture this, Christ was hanging on the cross, He would have been completely right, to point out our sins and the sins of the world but He laid it down His own rightness and kept His mouth shut. He chose in favor of drawing you close to win the world unto Himself through undeserved love via grace. He will love you while you are rejecting Him, how wondrous is His grace, because He first loved us. He first chooses us despite our yuck and stinking SIN. Thus, creating an environment that He could feed you the chain breaking truth that would set you free from that SIN. He could have spoken the truth and said, "Edward, you're a rotten sinner unworthy of my presence." But He drew me close, by shutting His mouth and **not** choosing His right to be right, He chose rather to be broken bread and poured out wine for my sake, drawing me in with my open heart to Him because of the Love He shows me despite my sin. **Jeremiah 31:3** He became the servant of all. He did not choose to be right even though He was, but rather to win us by wooing us close, in preference Saying **"forgive them Father for they do not know what they are doing."** This is what we Christ followers ought to say about others when they are in error and we see it and it bothers us. This is the complete opposite of the church world today everyone screaming for their rights "I am more correct than you are." Instead of us covering the faults of our brothers with love and prayer choosing the lower spot in hope to win them later by sowing seeds of truth. Let's face it, God brings us to situations in life to expose your heart condition. But I live more proactively and seek to chase after His Heart to make it mine through study of the word and obedience in the moment of exposure of my sin and error.

So often we want to speak the truth at the cost of a relationship, at the cost of love but Jesus did not think this way. He chooses to keep the relationship intact and speaks the truth when they are ready. He chooses love to dominate the relationship over Him being right.

Here is the proof:

John 16:12 (NKJV)

"I have many things to say to you but you are not ready to hear them."

John 3:12 (NKJV)

"If I have told you earthly things and you do not believe, how will you believe if I tell you heavenly things?"

When I use the word woo, I mean the drawing power of love and kindness. Just as it is written in **Jeremiah 31:3**. The recipient chooses to open their heart because of love. The soil is being readied with loving kindness; they have felt love from the giver which allows us to drop in everlasting seeds of truth into prepared fertile hearts. The love prepared human heart is the good soil of the hearer readied for the everlasting seed that never returns void of performance, is now alive and planted in them, Jesus Himself. **Matthew 13:23.**

So, being right about a doctrinal topic or a method of worship is not the point when it comes to how we walk with Christ and our brothers in Christ. Smashing people with your rightness or truth of understanding even if it is 100 percent correct, is not the way. "Speak the truth in LOVE," says the Lord. Love must be dominant not truth bashing and trashing. Remember **1 Corinthians 13, and 1 Corinthians 16:14** read it "If I have no love, I am nothing, I have failed." It is easy to be a bull in a China shop and wreck your relationships for the sake of truth especially anonymously on the internet but now you have lost them and they will never listen to you again. You walk away and saying, "I spoke truth" and feel good about it but you have lost the war while winning the battle. God gave me a wife for me to learn to love Gods way, to train me to love someone before myself. To learn to be careful with my words. To learn to value our loving relationship over me being right about a topic or thing.

My marriage relationship is more important to me than the truth I that could speak and cause damage to it, so I pray and wait for the due time. Is Christ, not the groom, and we are His bride? He is seeking relationship of intimacy over truth because He cannot help Himself but to love His bride, for He is love. If I am speaking to a sinner, do I look up Scripture to bash him over the head so that he would stop his sinful behavior? Or do I reveal to him with compassion in my heart the Love for God, restoring and rebuilding him to know the truth, revealing the path to God for him to follow alone, gently waiting for his desire to grow for Christ to grow and increase in Him? When Jesus is discovered by the sinner, he will willingly choose Jesus's ways of life, **Isaiah 55:8-9** and not his own sinful ways and the sin that Jesus hates, he will hate. This is true repentance; this is the changing of the heart and thinking of a person. Jesus sows everlasting seeds with love drenched water, the aim is good ground prepared with love and care for their hearts. **Mark 4** over and over we read, "Jesus had compassion on them." Meaning like a Father understanding the ignorance of the ways of his own children and still lovingly and caring for them. Always hopeful for them, drawing them in anticipations of Spiritual understanding knowing the seed will grow in their hearts someday. Blessed is He.

Jesus is the everlasting seed that never returns void of performance in the hearts of men. I have heard many teens and twenty somethings say to me over the years as a leader to them "I speak the truth no matter the situation" I am saying to you that love and care must precede your mouth or the truth you have will fall on stony ground. When I sow seed I want good soil, love prepared ground. This will avoid you giving pearls before swine, seeds of truth to the unready, unprepared un loved heart. Meaning you spoke truth but they were not ready for it and you wasted your everlasting seeds/pearls into rocky soil or an unready heart. You have wasted good seed on rocky soil. You over salted and ruined the meat. You gave a precious pearl of truth to someone that you have not prepared the ground on with Love and patience.

I was a garlic Farmer few years ago and you have to prepare the ground before you plant any cloves of seed. When I ready the soil with loving prep work like tilling and nutrients, the success and quality level rises massively in the garlic. Do I speak the truth with a hammer smashing my wife or kids and bruising their spirit? Or do I try to find a sweet gentile way to communicate the same truth into fertile love prepared soil? Think about your teen at home, do you speak every word that crosses your mind pushing them away as they walk out the door? It is best to wait until there is a moment of good soil between you to plant good seed. I focused on keeping the relationship between us intact with my wife or teen first as being paramount in my heart towards her vs me being right about topic or thing is secondary.

Jesus says, "**be the salt of the world**" and couch your expression to them to cause them to want MORE. Have you noticed, you cannot eat one salty potato chip, you want more. Sometimes we have to manage how much salt we use for a topic; the recipient may get burned up with too much salt at once. It is best to sprinkle God and truth in a conversation and as the salt is accepted sprinkle more and more as they are ready. This will allow you to practice patients in your communications with the ultimate desire is to deliver chain breaking truth in love which is a fruit of the spirit. **The recipient governs the amount of salt I use!** Think about that statement, Jesus treated me this very way when He presented salvation to me, Jesus patiently waited until I was ready. If He had presented salvation to me when I was not, the predictableness of my positive response would have been left to doubt. If a husband says to his wife, "You're FAT!" anyone with common sense knows that's not the way to sprinkle salt. Those words wound her tender soul. You take her by the hand lovingly and say let us go for a walk. The result is the same in aiding her to lose weight and preferring her and now your relationship is still intact so you can work on more stuff together with open hearts and fertile ground to work with. The recipient and the keeping of our relationship is more important to Christ and to me than me speaking the truth all at once with a hammer or dump truck. Truth is very important it sets men free but in the end, LOVE is more important it aids in the capacity for someone to receive the truth with understanding. Think on this a bit. **1 Corinthians 13, Ephesians 4:15** without love you have failed already says the word. Speak the truth in LOVE saints, love never fails, Jesus is love. Love is patient love is kind love aids in the capacity of the listener to receive the truth. Please embrace this!

I understand and have seen that truth sets men free but the truth should be delivered through the vessel of love. **1 Corinthians 16:14** Love has compassion for the ignorant and delivers truth at the time the seed will bear its best fruit when able. For some reason, we have not been taught that the different soil conditions of the hearts of men is the responsibility of the truth giver. **Matthew 13:8** If someone walks up to me and rebukes me for something and I do not know them at all, the effectiveness of the rebuke may likely fail because of the lack of love or relationship with me. This is more like a dive by shooting or dumping and running. But if a friend comes to me like David and Nathan, a true friend, and corrects me with truth and cares about what he is saying odds are very high it will be accepted. If I plant a garlic seed out of season, your results may vary even total failure but if you want predictability for increase returns like farmers do and God does, you do it at the right time of year with the right soil/heart conditions. Let's look at a teen, you can deliver truth dumped on them as they walk out the door and it does not penetrate the hard soil, the seed fell on hard or rocky soil and takes no root. But if you can express from their perspective, a loving and caring word to them they accept the seed and it grows without fail. Because of the law of sowing and reaping. Did Jesus present His salvation truth in you this very way? You understood Jesus loved you and your heart opened and it was ready because of His love and the seed of Salvation drops into your heart, with fertile soil and it took root evidenced by Godly change of thinking.

He did not save me when I was a child when I first heard of Him, I lacked understanding as a child for the need of abandonment of my own ways to choose His ways as savior, it was not understood by me yet. I had no concept of what trusting God meant at this time. He waited until I could choose Him with willing understanding of His way of salvation and I was willing to abandon my own ways of thinking for His. I understand now, God was wooing me at the age of nine years old. My sister got baptized at a church and the minister gave me a blue book of prayers. But salvation did not come to me until I figured out I needed something other than my sick sinning self, so Jesus waited for the right time. This happened when I was twenty-one-years old. James Robison was on TBN in June of 1981 and he ushered me into the kingdom. I was broken, my earthly Father had died when I was seventeen years old. I became a father to my son, which I was not ready for, at the age of eighteen. I had no job I had very little skills and no self-confidence, I was under tremendous stress. I was diagnosed with an ulcer because of the stress I was under. Here was the stumbling stone Jesus provided for me. It was either going to hide from my pain using drugs once more or let go and allow God to catch me. I had nowhere to turn but to God to save me, Blessed is HE. So, the wooing started when I was nine years old on a small boy's heart that wanted to know Him better reading the blue prayer book. He loved and wooed me for years but at the age of twenty-one I realized with understanding and a change of heart and thought, what He had done for me and what He would do now if I would TRUST HIM. I found freedom in HIM. I was not a saint folks, Jesus in the middle of my sin, while I still had the stinking smell of sin on me, He reached for me in the middle of my darkness and stole me from the gates of Hell and ignorance. Jesus brought me to the understanding of His work of His love and salvation I needed and I yielded to His truth and not mine, just at the right time. I was ready. I was bathed and overcome with His love, I cried at my salvation with tears flowing down my face. I remember because I knew He loved me, He over whelmed my sin with His love the victory of His shed blood and the work of the cross won my heart to His. Blessed is HE forever.

Colossians 4:6 (AMP)

Let your speech at all times be gracious and pleasant, seasoned with salt, so that you will know how to answer each one [who questions you].

Gracious and pleasant and seasoned words drew me to Him. His Love and Grace was understood by me and my heart opened and was ready. This enabled me to abandon my own ways for His ways. Salvation came to me with willingness to abandon my own ways of thought and understanding for His, because of love.

So, you have an opportunity to once more to salt and re-salt someone in your life, allow love to prepare the soil of their heart first. Let us look at the opposing view of this concept. You tell them the truth without love, you hurt them with it, the heart closes as a protection response and you never see them again, you are done. What did you gain? Jesus wants fruit increase, but you spoke the truth with no fruit, no love prep soil. Many want to speak the truth and not care if it brings forth fruit. The aim for them is to feeling good, "I told the truth." But Jesus command is to speak the truth in love. The seed fell on hard or rocky soil and did not take root. My goal is to sow good seed on good soil. Love, care, kindness prepares the soil it removes the rocks and weeds for good tilled fertile dirt for growth just like my garlic field. Read **Matthew 13:3-9 and 18-23** Love and kindness is soil prep, heart prep to receive the everlasting truth.

So, I listen to their voice, and look at their eyes to determine the heart condition in an individual on the fly. The eyes are the windows to the soul they can teach and tell you much. I drop truth in a measure that the Spirit leads me, did the seed fall on good soil I ponder? Was the salt received willingly? If they were able to manage what I gave them, I give a bit more. If not, I back off and continue with love and kindness so I maintain the opportunity to sow again and again in them. If you look into their eyes, they will tell you if the word of truth landed on good or unprepared soil. Saints, have mercy and grace, compassion for the ignorant ones around you no matter how much the ignorant may think they know or how much it bothers you. Jesus did this for you, did He not? Were you not ignorant of His saving love, did He give you His grace Mercy and compassion when you needed it, despite your sinful ignorance and resistance? He waited to drop the good seed or salt when you were ready. He waited on your heart to sow seed to fall on good soil, to open a fertile heart. His word never returns void of performance. We ought to do the same for those that God has given us, so follow Christ! Before I speak to any crowd, I ask the Lord to prepare the hearts of the listeners to receive the good seed, Jesus, the good Word of God to be sown in them on good soil. I have even asked the Lord to pluck up seeds I planted mistakenly because of some error or sin on my part. The love and compassion I have for them precedes the seed, just like Jesus did. The love that fills my heart to give to others comes from Him. Jesus stood on a hill with tears in His eyes while looking for His children's ready hearts but they rejected and forsook Him as truth, He had compassion for the ignorance in them with tears. For without Him I can do nothing but with Him I can do all things. Love wins in sowing truth in the hearts of men!

1 Corinthians 13:1-3 (AMP)

If I speak with the tongues of men and of angels, but have not love then I have become only a noisy gong or a clanging cymbal [just an annoying distraction].... 3b But if I have not LOVE, it profits me nothing.

Wow, listen to this Christian leaders, if I raise the dead, heal the sick, have all revelational truth even preach the gospel to all the world but I have NO love in my heart for them, I have wasted my time and have lost my reward with God even though I had truth. This reveals something, we need to take a second look at Church. LOVE, the care and kindness I have for my brothers are more important than everything even if I am right about a truth God has given me. I think the church at large ignores this issue because it is so hard and yet so simple to implement. It requires the picking up of your cross that Christians have forgotten on the ground. **Luke 14:27, John 13:35.**

John 13:34 Jesus Speaking

"I am giving you a new commandment, that you love one another. Just as I have loved you, so you too are to love one another."

How did God love me, with mercy, grace, and compassion not giving me what I deserved [mercy] and often giving me what I did not deserve [Grace]? For some reason, we will not do that for our Christian brothers or even those outside of the church world. Jesus said in **John 13:35** the outside world, the unbelievers would know I was a Christ follower by how I loved and cared for my Christian brothers inside the church. Being the last days you would think we would be more mature in Christ yet we need to feed the milk the elementary teaching of love once again.

If we want revival in our nation, we must do **John 13:34-35** in the church first then outside. Compassion, grace, and mercy should fill and over flow our hearts, our churches or How will the outsider, unbeliever Know that I am in Christ but by the love I show to my brothers in this world. **Luke 14:27, John 13:35** Think on this!

James 4:11-12 (AMP)

11 Believers, do not speak against or slander one another. He who speaks [self-righteously] against a brother or judges his brother [hypocritically], speaks against the Law and judges the Law. If you judge the Law, you are not a doer of the Law but a judge of it.

V11 Read this in the KJV it is a hard one. Here is James, again discipleship training class.

12 There is only one Lawgiver and Judge, the One who is able to save and to destroy [the one God who has the absolute power of life and death]; but who are you to [hypocritically or self-righteously] pass judgment on your neighbor?

John 3:17, Luke 6:37 confirms the above scripture Christ has not come to judge or be a critic at this time and neither are we. But we are to esteem others higher than ourselves even if we do not agree with them. Am I building people and the church or tearing it down? Jesus was always building brick upon brick from faith to faith ever building the kingdom of His Father on earth, Jesus is the chief cornerstone. The question is, am I gathering or am I scattering? Christ came to build the kingdom and to bring His Fathers will down from heaven, the question is, are you? We are to follow and do what He did? You can use the WORD of God to scrutinize out doctrine but once you point your finger at a person or bring in his/her name or identified a people group you have sinned; you have broken the Love of Christ you are no longer building or gathering.

It is Satan working at his best at being the **accuser of the brethren** with your mouth and His Church. **Revelation 12:10, John 10:27, Luke 6:31-37** who are you following, and who are you acting like when you have accused or gossip about your brothers or neighbor in this way, even if you are right? O Lord please forgive us our ignorance!

Luke 6:37 Jesus Speaking

37 "Judge not, and you shall not be judged. Condemn not, and you shall not be condemned. Forgive, and you will be forgiven."

In other words, sow love, and how is love manifested by grace, mercy, and compassion it is like a seed, sow forgiveness into the hearts of ignorant men. Do not take offense but overlook a fault, offence or error, and you will reap the same from the Lord. Live with your cup overflowing with grace, mercy, and compassion to all those that the Lord has given you. Living for Christ will give you abundance of opportunities to take offence and hurt but love over comes sin. Love that you may also reap the same Love planted. I need all the mercy, grace, and compassion I can get, how about you? **1 Corinthians 13.**

Everything in this world belongs to Christ says **Psalms 24:1** whether you like it or not. This makes Jesus the Master over all. **Psalms 89:11** I will not judge the servant of my Master, every one of us is His and He will deal with the good and faithful and those that are not, it is not my place. **Proverbs 30:10** All of creation will render to Jesus the Master an account of their lives in and out of Christ. Lord, I pray that you keep me, that I may never sit in the seat of judgement, for the world and everyone in it belongs to you alone. **Romans 14:11.**

Read **1 Corinthians 6:1-7 (AMP)** We bring shame to the church body when Christian disagreements are exposed to the unbelieving world, verbally or blasting someone on the internet or TV, this is to our SHAME and is SIN. It is like taking your wife's or husband's deepest shameful discrepancies on to the internet for the world to see your dishonor.

Any Ministry that does this, I avoid and treat it as a sign from the Lord, I mark them to not being contaminated even though I need them in my life. I will pray for them from a distance and ask for their repentance to be revealed in them like a priest would have compassion on ignorance of His people. Or a parent that has compassion on the ignorance of their children. Always in love and kindness because of mercy and grace God has been given me. If I am able to speak to them one on one, I will. May God's grace be with me to confront gently, and sow good seed otherwise I shut my mouth and keep it in prayer for God is able, He is the MASTER of the hearts of Men. I am proof of that.

Proverbs 30:10 (NKJV)

Do not malign a servant to his master, lest he curse you, and you be found guilty

Why, be the critic of your master's servant, there is no LOVE mercy or grace in it? Flee from sin and hate it. Then you also have sown seeds you can't afford to reap them. Your eyes are on others and their weakness and not on God. **Luke 14:15-24** When we take our eyes off God we start to eat from the tree of good and evil because we think we have a good and better way. But God wants our eyes fixed on Him eating from the tree of life and Love. Keep your eyes on God and not on the waves of circumstance that will cause you to sink and sin. Please understand brothers and sisters ponder this!

Philippians 2:3 (AMP)

3 Do nothing from selfishness or empty conceit [through factional motives, or strife], but with [an attitude of] humility [being neither arrogant nor self-righteous], regard others as more important than yourselves.

If I regard others as more important than myself, how can I render a criticism or fault finding of my brother speck while hosting a beam in my own eye? You can't, but take the beam out of your own eye first Edward. **Romans 2:1-3 (AMP)** Dear saint, the Lord has granted you to judge the fruit of their works only. The individual is a servant of the Lord Master and it is not your place to render a critical opinion of them, like the world does. The individual belongs to the Master and He will deal with them in due time. **Jeremiah 17:10**.

I also do not wait to forgive someone, waiting for an apology or some kind of sorrow or remorse on their part but I give it without their asking quickly. Jesus gave me aggressive forgiveness and died on the cross while I was still His enemy. Saying, "Father, forgive them, for they do not know what they do" **Luke 23:34**.

If you study this verse, He is forgiving me for my ignorance and corresponding foolish sinful actions before I realized I needed forgiveness while I was working against Him and rejecting Him like an enemy. We ought to do the same with others, forgiving them and not waiting for them to have understanding or have sorrow of an offence done unto us. You giving something like forgiveness before they even deserve or ask for it, it is the exercise of GRACE working in you. "Because this is God's Love working and enabled you to overlook a fault." He has done it for us, then I must do it for others. Sow the seed of forgiveness do not wait a moment more!

Matthew 7:16a

16 You will <u>know them by their fruits</u>. Do men gather grapes from thornbushes or figs from thistles?

Is what that person or ministry is doing, building the church, drawing the wayward prodigals to Christ, renewing the fire of the cold-hearted, redeeming the unbelievers for Jesus Christ and His kingdom? Are what others are doing, following Christ's example or is what they are doing being modeled in God's word? Remember, study what is good and you will know what is evil. These are the things I ponder and can judge by fruit, but no further. I do not follow the blind into a ditch. I will not eat from the tree of good and evil, the tree of opinion. I do not gossip or render opinions about other ministries or persons. I walk after Christ the best I can and if others follow me great, if not, great. My place is to act like Him, follow Him, love like Him FIRST, the rest second. I chase after love and chase after Him for God is love, living His way is love and victory over this life. When I minister I do so in support of something like doctrinal truth or teaching of Holiness not against an identified someone's doctrinal error or denomination. Some say I am chicken to take on topics of sin with in the church. But if I teach you to love Christ and seek Him in prayer and in the word, holiness will take root in you thus producing good fruit that you can examine. Even this document is a teaching of Holiness and truth lifting the standard of Christ in you the hope for the world. Jesus, when on the mount, spoke of the standard of godliness read **Matthew 5** and **Luke 6:20-49** he did not spend any time slamming sinners for their broken dysfunction but He lifted a new standard for them to desire and hope in. So, I take Jesus as a model and copy and do as he did and following Him walking as He walked. I lift up holiness and righteousness and Jesus, Himself, so that others may do, copy and follow and repeat.

I serve God by serving God's people the best way I know and drawing them closer to Jesus Christ and teaching and training them in His ways of thinking. Which is repentance revealed when we change to HIS ways and not our ways of thinking and thus living. His thoughts and ways are higher than our thoughts and ways **Isaiah 55:8-9.**

I measure and examine the fruit if it does the same building, lifting, and restoring. **Jeremiah 17:10** I have compassion for the ignorant, of those that have misunderstandings of Jesus's ways, not judgement, I desire to draw them close if able so that I may build others unto Christ and His ways of thinking. "Preach the Gospel and teach them My ways of thinking," says Jesus. **Matthew 28:18-20, Mark 16:15-16, Luke 14:15-24.**

When we judge folks, we erect walls and obstacles, the woo is broken, the drawing power to the kingdom is broken, the compelling compassion of God is broken. **Jeremiah 31:3** and it creates disunity from us touching their hearts for Christ, you have lost the opportunity already because of your desire to be right and superior to others or greater than them. But Jesus asked you to be the servant of all, choose the lower spot saints. You have sown judgment and now you will soon reap it if repentance or a change of thought does not occur in your heart quickly. **Romans 2:1-3 NKJ, Jeremiah 17:10, Ecclesiastes 12:14.**

Jesus always loved the people, and it was written He had compassion for them which resulted in miracles. I wonder if that is a clue to me that love and compassion that I received from God proceeds the move of God.

1 John 2:9 (AMP)

9 The one who says he is in the Light [in consistent fellowship with Christ] and yet habitually hates (works against) his brother [in Christ] is in the darkness until now.

Wow, you are done here Edward, this verse says it all. There is no room for you to be your brother's critic only to woo him or her with love and kindness so that you may win them to Christ again and again with his salt, seeds, water of loving truth. **Jeremiah 31:3** Jesus is not interested in you being right or being the winner or correct but for you to learn to love and be the servant of them all. It is and has always been about the exposer your heart condition which equals sanctification working in you.

Jesus is not interested in you eating from the tree of good and evil but He is desiring for you to eat from the tree of LIFE that requires the laying down of your rightness in preference to love, mercy, and grace. Love never fails. Jesus never fails, Jesus is love. Will you choose to live this way? Love, woos your brothers to everlasting truth that will set them Free from darkness. It is HARD work to do this I realize, this is why they call it picking up your cross and keeping your mouth shut, it is hard to do, there is suffering in it, willingly pick up your cross and follow Him saints. This is the inner court, this is discipleship, this is the denial of self and picking up your cross and follow His ways and forsake you own ways.

I Corinthians 12:25-27 (AMP)

25 so that there would be no division or discord in the body [that is, lack of adaptation of the parts to each

other], but that the parts may have the same concern for one another. 26 And if one member suffers, all the parts share the suffering; if one member is honored, all rejoice with it. 27 Now you [collectively] are Christ's body, and individually [you are] members of it [each with his own special purpose and function].

If we are in Christ's Body, we should not be about antagonistic behaviors to people to the other parts of the body but prefer rather to be builders and displayers of God's service and love through grace and mercy.

Opinions verbalized that are birthed because of differences or my own rightness, is a display of immaturity and does not come from the Lord and the tree of life but from the tree of good and evil. Think on this!

We should only correct a brother in person face to face, one on one, and my concern should be for him and his wellbeing while doing so, they are more important than the correction I bring, if not, keep your mouth shut because your heart is not ready.

Jesus does this with us, does He not? While maintaining the relationship between us, no matter what happens even if we stray in our error into sin, He loves and bathes us in love. There is no drive-by rebuking or dump and run allowed in the kingdom. We correct a brother and stick with that brother because Jesus first loved us and did the same for us when He found us in our own ignorant error filled situation. Did Jesus correct you of all ignorance when you found salvation or drop a dump truck load all over you about your sin? He did not, He draws you with His love, mercy, and grace waiting for you to willingly submitted to His LOVE to hear His truth that set you free from darkness, ignorance and lies.

You willingly give up your sin from your fisted grip. So it is with us we come alongside a brother in love and care and aid him in better understanding of who Christ is. Discipleship is not the business of the faint-hearted it will take work and much effort and the death of your arrogant self to do the work. Did Jesus submit to the Father and worked with twelve guys of different sinful characters and discover that it was fun times for Him? I bet it was not, it was work, effort on His part with patience and tolerance, He may have wanted to smash some heads at times. He laid down being right in preference to winning them to His Fathers ways of thinking. Think on this. Remember you do not have the right to be right to set yourself above your brothers or another but only the right to be the servant of them all and choose the lower spot and carry your cross and deny your own self nature and follow Him and eat from the tree of life. Remember for as a man thinks in his heart so is he, in his doings. It is not what goes in the man that corrupts a man but what comes out of him. **Matthew 15:11.**

Isaiah 54:17 (KJV)

17 No weapon that is formed against thee shall prosper; and every tongue that shall rise against thee in judgment thou shalt condemn. This is the heritage of the servants of the Lord, and their righteousness is of me, saith the Lord.

V17b It is just me? I do not want to be on the other side of this verse. I want to be found by Christ being His servant, friend of the Lord, how about You?

Every tongue, critic, backbiter, or opinion rendered aloud shall render to the Lord an account for every idle word to Christ Himself, think on this! Every word we speak! It is a fearful thing to land in the hands of the Lord.

Matthew 12:36 (NKJV)

36 But I say to you that for every idle word men may speak; they will give account of it in the day of judgment.

I Peter 2:1 AMP (NKJV)

So put aside every trace of meanness and all deceit and hypocrisy and envy and all slander and hateful speech;

Pray for your enemies, love everyone and esteem others higher than yourself and you will do well. Know that the Lord shall repay the wicked MOUTH for every word. Because you do not see it happening *now* you complain internally. But Read **Ecclesiastes 8:11 KJV, Matthew 12:36**.

Pick up your cross and proclaim with your voice and heart **"forgive them for they do not know what they are doing"** when critics arise against you, excuse their ignorance and take no offence you have just sown mercy.

Ecclesiastes 8:11 (KJV)

11 Because sentence against an evil work is not executed speedily, therefore the heart of the sons of men is fully set in them to do evil.

Imagine if God were to deal out your reward for every evil word or work instantly like a lightning bolt, no one would sin. The choice not to SIN would be taken away from you. For "Sin is pleasurable for a moment but around the corner comes unseen, what we have sown." In the Middle of SIN is "i." The self-nature in us can be studied in Romans 8. This "i" must die for us to be Holy even as He is Holy. We are Holy and set apart positionally but now we work out our salvation with fear and trembling **Philippians 2:12** Adam, Eve, and Jesus were all tempted and Satan was their appealing to the "i" in them. To the "i" and our self-nature in us all. Read it and take note of it. Satan appeals to the "i" in you, that is the fruit form the tree of good and evil. Be set apart saints eat from the tree of Life, be Holy and set apart for His use, pick up the cross that you left on the ground and be broken bread, be poured out wine that celebrates and anoints others to do the same to follow Christ's ways. **Leviticus 20:7, 1 Peter 1:15-16.**

James 1:14 (NKJV)

But each one is tempted when he is drawn away by his own desires and enticed.

It is the "i" in us all, the self-nature that is enticed away to sin. This is why the elder body needs to yield to the younger born again spirit in us. The Spirit of God in us needs to increase and our self-nature the sinful "i" needs to decrease work it out.

Proverbs 10:19 (NKJV)

In the multitude of words, sin is not lacking, But he who restrains his lips is wise.

In light of **Matthew 12:36** it is best to confine one's words to building and not tearing down. To build someone, get out of the habit of **opinion rendering** which is eating from the wrong tree. To do this you will learn to yield to Christ in you. This is the denying of self-nature and the picking up of the cross. Your mind runs to be the critic because you are determining if something is good and evil then you open your mouth and render opinion. We ought not to eat from the tree of good and evil, Satan's trick is to get us to render an opinion which results in SIN and much speaking. We should eat only from the tree of LIFE, its fruit are slathered with love that has mercy and grace in the meat of it. Train yourself to examine in thought but to refrain from immediate speech. This is one of the Cross lessons I walk with daily even today after walking with Christ for over forty-one years. **James 1:19** The word says in **James 1:19** be "Quick to listen and slow to speak and even slower to wrath." The hearts of men and following their mouth is desperately wicked if not yielded to Christ. **Jeremiah 17:9.**

Ephesians 4:29 (NJKV)

29 Let no corrupt word proceed out of your mouth, but what is good for necessary edification, that it may impart grace to the hearers.

Oh My Lord, awaken your church to this concept. Grant us a willingness to submit to your word, O Lord. For our hearts are wicked and without you we are doomed. But with You O Mighty God we are able to do great and mighty things. **Jeremiah 17:9.**

Awaken the bride to cleanse herself and to make herself clean and ready for you my Lord, for the groom will soon appear to collect her. O bride of God, humble yourself now, no one can do it for you. **James 4:10** You must choose it yourself, it is your own doing. You must lay down your old ways and choose His ways. You must pick up your own cross and deny yourself nature, no one can do it for you. **Luke 9:23** Please, O Lord, have mercy and awaken this truth in the hearts of those that are called by your Name. Remember your loving kindness, O Lord, even when we have not been loving and kind. Remember your faithfulness even when we have not been faithful. **Jeremiah 31:3.**

Proverbs 16:28 (NKJV)

A perverse man sows strife and discord, And a whisperer separates the best of friends.

If you sow discord or division between brothers, you have sinned. Then you will also reap what you have sown as well. This is why Jesus said "go to your brother and make things right one on one **first** before you bring an offering… to Me." **Matthew 5:22-24, 18:15-17 AMP.** I have been here and have done this to my own shame, Lord, pluck up those sown seeds and forgive me my ignorance.

WRONG TARGET

Jesus rebuked Satan influencing Peter, let me show you. When Satan used Peter to tell Jesus he would not allow Him to be crucified. Jesus knew who His enemy was, not the broken misguided Peter or people, but the deception of Satan working in Peter. **Matthew 16:23** This is why Jesus says pray for your enemies, in this case Peter. His fight is not with flesh and blood. His fight was not with Peter, it was with Satan and his deceptions working in him. Read **2 Corinthians 10:3-5.**

Matthew 5:22-24 (AMP)

22 But I say to you that everyone who continues to be angry with his brother or harbors malice against him shall be guilty before the court; and whoever speaks [contemptuously and insultingly] to his brother, ...23 So if you are presenting your offering at the altar, and while there you remember that your brother has something [such as a grievance or legitimate complaint] against you, 24 leave your offering there at the altar and go. First make peace with your brother, and then come and present your offering .....

Proverbs 13:10 (AMP)

Through pride and presumption comes nothing but strife and discord, But [skillful and Godly] wisdom is with those who welcome [well-advised] counsel.

Will you prefer your brother even if you are right biblically while keeping your mouth shut? Remember you do not have the right to be right but to be broken bread poured out wine for His use. The Lord uses you as He wills and it is not about you wining, it is not about you being right, but it is about maintaining the relationship so you and I can speak into their hearts of others again and again bring them along into all truth. Jesus teaching is one on one and it is always about revealing your heart condition. Proof of this is Jesus did this with me and you before our salvation. He could have said your rotten to the bone depart from me Edward, but He reached out to my sinful rotten self while I was rejecting Him and salted, and seeded me when I needed it over and over again until I became the man He intended me to be. **His focus is not who I am today sinful, broken but what I will become for Him tomorrow, Holy.** These are Gods eyes; may I see with them O Lord give me your eyes. Think about the fisherman Peter. broken and rotten and Jesus saying to him, "Come and Follow me. We need to be about the same work."

Follow me Edward even though you have sin in your life Jesus said this to Peter and to the world, follow me do as I do. God hates sin but is willing to overlook it in you to win you to himself, can you see it. Oh, know I just ruffled some feathers. Be a woo-er of men, drawer of men, compeller of men to come and know ME better, says Jesus. Read **Jeremiah 31:3** Do you think the twelve disciples were fun for Christ to WORK with daily, all their dysfunction and bickering, sin, lack of faith, and inexperience? Do you think He could have said to them get out of here you stinking sinner or did He draw them with Enduring Kindness and Patience the fruit of the spirit to later salt, seed feed water them again and again over and over in hope?

Loving truth is caring for another in truth. Truth is more easily digested and gets rid of "stinken thinken" and draws men in for more, loving truth. "For as a man thinks in his heart so is he" in his actions. Jesus had loving thoughts and goals in HIS heart concerning me, you and the world. He had a goal in mind and tolerated our ineptness, sin on my part because He was looking at what I will become, more than what I was rotten. So, He could drop in more chain breaking loving truth into my ready to receive soil and loved on heart. **Proverbs 10:19.**

Something to consider: all those in the Hall of Fame in the book of Hebrews 11 they had sin and flaws in them but God was focused on what they and us the descendants would be in the future and not on their present sinful situations. We all need to see people as He see them. We need to see them with His eyes of FAITH, hope and love. Hoping blessing that they may arrive to the destiny planed out for them our hope is Christ in them. Now let's go back to sowing and reaping for a bit. If I live thinking and hoping the best in folks, blessing, loving, hoping, caring, praying for them then what have I sown for myself? I rejoice in suffering in my flesh nature for Christ? Because I bounce back hiding in Him being more than a conqueror and overcomer in Christ. Do you see it?

1 Corinthians 9:19-23 (NKJV) Paul says he becomes all things for the sake of the gospel v19a, 23. Paul lays down His right to be right for the sake of wining others to Christ. Paul will do what it takes without SINNING to compel folks to Know Christ. Think on this. **Jeremiah 31:3** says the same about God, He woos folks, compels folks, loves without ceasing folks into the salvation of God and the better understanding of Himself and His truth. We have been modeled by Jesus and Paul by example these scriptures and more, should we model this to others as we walk in Christ? Both Corinthians and Jeremiah verses here illustrate a willingness to patiently win the ignorant of understanding with loving truth. Both scriptures illustrate a patient reach out with love and sacrifice before truth. The heart of ignorant man is waiting to receive its eternal truth seed that will set them free from darkness and chains of sin. But love prepares the ground for the good seed to fall into. Speak the truth in love. Do you see it yet?

Galatians 6:1 (AMP)

Brothers, if anyone is caught in any sin, you who are spiritual [that is, you who are responsive to the guidance of the Spirit] are to restore such a person in a spirit of gentleness [not with a sense of superiority or self-righteousness], keeping a watchful eye on yourself, so that you are not tempted as well.

This is what we ought to be doing, this sums up this lesson nicely. Is it a nice feeling that if a spiritual One finds a fault in you he will lovingly address it with you alone? He will address it with you one on one and never shame and blast you on the internet or in front of others about your error in thinking. If he cannot get a hold of you then he will lovingly pray for you and leave the matter up to the Spirit. **1 Peter 1:2, 2 Thessalonians 2:13, AMP,** that will be the end of it. Is that not a great feeling, The spiritual One is not trashing you behind your back. These above behaviors are what Christ has done for us, is it not? Then we ought to do the same to others.

Restore folks in teachableness, patience, loving-kindness, care, peace, and joy. Keeping the relationship is more important than correcting someone because you think you are more right. My friends wait until they are ready…. And pray for their readiness **Galatians 5:22-25, Matthew 5:9 (AMP)**

As a Man Thinks in His Heart So is He

REPENT

When God says REPENT, He is saying change the way you think and choose His way of thinking over your own ways of thinking for His ways and thoughts are higher than yours. Read Isaiah 55:8-9.

Saying "I am sorry" about a topic is not repentance, acting and thinking and living differently **is** the fruit of repentance. As a parent, you do not want to hear, "I am sorry" from your kids but you want them to act differently and do differently. How you act or respond is key "you shall know them by the fruit" This is huge. Do you remember Jesus speaking about two guys? He told them to do something. One said, he would and did not do what was requested and the other said he would not but did it later. Jesus said the one that DID the work is the one rewarded. It is in the doing we see repentance. Not in the verbal shallow "I am sorry." **Matthew 7:24.**

Matthew 7:24 (NKJV)

24 "Therefore whoever hears these sayings of Mine, and does them, I will liken him to a wise man who built his house on the rock:

What is it that proves my repentance, my thoughts have changed my corresponding actions because **"For as a man thinks in his heart so is he"** in his actions.

Romans 2:4 (AMP)

Or do you have no regard for the wealth of His kindness and tolerance and patience [in withholding His wrath]?

Are you [actually] unaware or ignorant [of the fact] that God's kindness leads you to repentance [that is, to change your inner self, your old way of thinking—seek His purpose for your life]?

Here God reveals that it is His love, mercy, and kindness just as **Jeremiah 31:3** says that leads us to repentance a change of mind thus a change of life and actions. Would it be a stretch to say if we show love, mercy, grace, and kindness to the unbelieving world and to our brothers in Christ that it would draw them to repentance and a changed mind and as a result their actions? Please read **Jeremiah 31:3-4** What happened to those that understood God's love and kindness, they changed for as a man thinks in His heart so is he....in his actions.

Proverbs 23:7a (NKJV)

For as a man thinks in his heart, so is he.

Jesus is challenging us to think like Him, to live dependently upon God like He did unto His Father, act like Him respond to the world like Him. This is big faith. So, if I change your thinking, **John 5:19** I am enabling you to repent or follow after Him and His likeness according to the word of truth. If we follow God and lean hard in dependency upon Him, His likeness will shine through you as His Father shown through Him. Jesus said if you have seen Me how can you say you have not seen the Father, we are ONE? This is my goal. **John 14:7-11.**

How do I start to think and live like Him?

To begin, I read the Bible as it was written to me directly, it is not about others or on their stuff. It is never about what others are or are not doing when it comes to walking with Christ in my view. The Word of God is focused like a laser, its target is on ME my own Heart and Mind and my own stuff because it is all that I control. READ **Psalms 119:1-24**. You can control only yourself and not others so this keeps your eyes on your own junk and not others. But the fruit of the Spirit is **self-control** so it is about How I respond and react to my daily interactions with folks and God in my life moment by moment. My responsibilities are my responses to live surrendered to him and to the lot in life God has given me. It is always about what Christ wants to do in me, in my heart, by me yielding to His ways over my own ways this is a dependent posture He seeks and is also abiding in the vine and eating from the tree of Life. **Isaiah 55:8-9** His kingdom come in ME as it is in heaven. It is Not about what is or is not happening in others' lives. God uses the lot in life, your situation the pains of your life, the broken parts to expose and bring out the wickedness in your own heart. Yield to Him the master of the hearts of men being aware always He is there with me all the time and being sensitive not to grieve Him because I love Him even when life hurts. He walks with me Hand in Hand, how Glorious. **Psalms 25.**

As a Man Thinks in His Heart So is He

SANCTIFICATION: THE INNER COURT

This is pretty much the opposite of a popular movement years ago that teaches "it is not about you." It is true when you think about the outer court life Jesus did it all without us. The inner court and discipleship and sanctification is all about you working cooperatively with the Holy Spirit. You learning to be a yielded vessel of obedience unto Him. When you read a Bible verse we have read here in this lesson He is talking all about YOU. **My sins are my own, my salvation is my own, my cross is my own and the Lord commands for me are my own, my time and intimacy with Him is my own, weather I go to heaven or hell is my own, I stand before Him and His throne on my own.** I live it, I teach it, I love it and share it with others So God can be their own. When Jesus tells you to love, to whom is God speaking to… YOU. The point is Jesus wants your heart and He wants us to learn to desire His heart. So it is all about YOU yielded to Him, shining Him, giving Him away to others and the Glory for all of it, is His alone. It is His righteousness and not our own. It is His heart and mind taking supremacy in you not our own, **Isaiah 55:8-9** O How Glorious. Forever the Glory is His alone.

Now is the time to magnify Jesus

I love to journal. My prayers in my prayer time, it is the biggest way to grow fast in Christ in my forty-one years of walking with Christ I have seen it duplicated in others as well. These writings here are from such journals. If you desire to hear God's voice the fastest way to develop that ear is to journal your prayers. If Christ means anointed one, and Christian means "Little Christ." Little anointed ones. Should we act Like Him, think like Him, love like Him, walk in FAITH like Him, change the world like Him? All this while thinking like Him to love others into His truth like Him. To live dependent on God, like Him. **John 5:30, 15:4-5 Philippians 4:13.**

What to Do Now?
Be Like Christ!
Kingdom Living Here and Now

Ephesians 5:1 (AMP)

Therefore, become imitators of God [copy Him and follow His example], as well-beloved children [imitate their father];

To whom is He speaking to... YOU... He is speaking directly to me and you, it is not about how others are or are not following Christ. It is ALL about you keeping your eyes and your mind on Him the author and finisher of your faith that grants us peace. It has never been about your eyes being on your brothers or neighbors' junk, stay out of their backyards.

Hebrews 6:12 (AMP)

...so that <u>you</u> will not be [spiritually] sluggish, but [will instead be] imitators of those who through faith [lean on God with absolute trust and confidence in Him and in His power] and by patient endurance [even when suffering] are [now] inheriting the promises.

O Lord, do not delay I hunger for your presence give me the promises to find you, bless me indeed that I may not harm but bring You honor and glory forever.

John 14:31 (AMP) Jesus Speaking

31 but so that the world may know [without any doubt] that I love the Father, I do exactly as the Father has

commanded Me [and act in full agreement with Him and His word]. Get up, let us go from here.

Now, if I may boldly say these above scriptures you should speak them about yourself in this self-same manner. Would you believe it? Now that you have been crushed and ground down by the stone, Jesus and His word and your soul has felt the sword piercing, Jesus says shake it off and "Get UP and let's go." From this point to holiness towards thinking as He thinks. Live in the higher thoughts and ways of Christ as beloved children of God. **Ephesians 5:1.**

Jesus follows His Father in perfect agreement, walking hand in hand doing His Father's will, in harmony of purpose, will you do the same? Jesus was a 100% MAN of faith meaning He lived in a life-dependent reliant posture upon the father, modeling how we should live dependent and trusting on the Spirit. Jesus demonstrates dependence, trust and reliance as a child upon His Father. David, Asa, and other prophets of old were successful when they live dependently and reliant upon God and not so successful when they veered off the path. Read **2 Chronicles 15:2,8, Hebrews 6:12.**

Now we are in the **Chain of Command** with Christ in His army. The Father, Jesus, the Spirit then us. Jesus is in submission to the Father, the spirit in submission to Jesus, and now you and I to live yielded, in glorious submission to the Spirit of God that will lead us and teach us all things everyone at the same time at different levels. Do you see the chain? Read **John 5:30, 12:26, 14:26, 15:26, 15:4-5.**

This is why the kingdom of God is taken by force, work, effort and struggle. It was never meant to be easy because the elder body must serve the younger born again spirit in me. The Spirit in me must increase and the self-nature the "i" in me must decrease. See **1 Corinthians 15:46, Genesis 25:23, Romans 9:12.** Here is the struggle, I do not believe in passive Christianity if you're not paddling hard to go upstream to know God, you are floating downstream in the same direction as the world. You are stuck in the outer court of the temple of God. Think on this.

FAITH

Luke 18:15-17 (AMP)

Now they were also bringing their babies to Him, so that He would touch and bless them, and when the disciples noticed it, they began reprimanding them. But Jesus called them to Himself, saying [to the apostles], "Allow the children to come to Me, and do not forbid them, for the kingdom of God belongs to such as these. I assure you and most solemnly say to you, whoever does not receive the kingdom of God [with faith and humility] like a child will not enter it at all."

The Spirit showed me something about children and faith, trust and humility in this verse, what are the circumstances that the children find themselves subconsciously in relation to their parents or those that care for them?

Ephesians 5:1

Therefore be imitators of God as dear children.

Dress me, cloth me, protect me, train me, teach me, forgive me, love me, care for me show me kindness and mercy and grace. This is how children live and thrive with respect to their parents, is it not? This is not even a complete list. Do you see the dependency, trust of the child on the parent? Our Father in heaven wants us to act and live in Him this very same way with trust and humility IN Him. Dress me, cloth me, protect me, train me, teach me, forgive me, love me, care for me show me kindness and mercy and grace. To enter His kingdom while on earth, we must live in DEPENDANCY, trust and reliance just as a child is dependent on their parent. This in turn make us humble because we do not depend on our own self efforts. Like a child, we live dependent trusting upon the spirit He has given us. My parent will clothe me and feed me without me thinking about it. This is FAITH a walk of dependence, trust, reliance upon Him just as He did with His Father. Do you see it? Think about the hall of famers of Hebrews 11. Without God they were all nothings but with Him they did great things.

In **John 5:30** Jesus proclaims He only does the Fathers will, He does no-thing without His Father's motives and He is sensitive to His Father's presence and His desire is to please His Father always. Read **John 15:4-5 Philippians 4:13** in these verses Jesus says follow ME do as I do and did. Now we have been modeled to do the same as Jesus did in **John 5:30**. We walk and follow after Christ's example; being led by the spirit of God that teaches and leads us into all truth. Being aware He is there and sensitive not to grieve Him.

When you do not know what to do, be loving to another. You cannot grieve God responding to someone in LOVE. Love never fails! Think on this….**1 Corinthians 13**.

How do I do it?

John 10:27 (NKJV)

My sheep hear My voice, and I know them, and they follow Me.

Three parts to this Verse.

1. **My sheep hear My voice**…We must learn to hear His voice ASAP see above how-tos.
2. **He knows Me**, meaning we are in relationship we both give our most valuable asset to one another, our time. You must get into Prayer life and the word it is just a must do.

3. **They follow Me**. I, in humility choose Him over myself, I yield to the Spirit that is in me to learn, to follow and to obey. Doing Psalms 1 and 119.

Jesus is saying, "I speak to my sheep" why not perk up your ears to hear Him. "They do as I do." We do the same and follow Christ in agreement with Him and His word, hand in hand the best we can. We have to learn to hear His voice. This comes via study of His word and prayer times, journaling helps a lot I do not know another way to get it quick. Prayer journals help reveal to you that it was God speaking to you on some certain date. You discover how to discern Him over your own thoughts. Follow after Him, act like Him, think like Him, live dependently upon God the Father like Him. Saints live dependently upon Him for without Him "you can do no-thing" but "with Him you can do all things." On your own, you can do no-thing not even breathe or blink your eye. Nothing of kingdom value or eternal value happens unless we abide in Him, follow Him. **John 5:30** Christ can do no-thing on His own, how much less can you? As you walk, you must be attentive to the spirit, focused upon Him not to grieve Him. Allow Him to guide you and speak to you in all loving truth. **Ephesians 4:30.**

Christ lived dependently upon His Father teaching us what faith looks like a dependent posture, which is trust and reliance on God **John 5:30** it shows us we are to live dependently trusting upon Christ to walk even as He walked in Faith, Trust and Loving dependency on the Father is faith.

1 John 2:6 (NKJV)

He who says he abides in Him ought himself also to walk just as He walked.

Jesus was 100% man of faith meaning He lived dependently on His chain of command, His Father. **John 5:30** Jesus said "yes" to His Father in the garden and in His life daily on earth. We all need to do the same. Do you see it yet?

This will stretch your faith; trust and you will grow fast in Him. Mark down the day and try this and you will be blown out of your socks seeing Him move through you strangely at first but effective for the kingdom.

John 5:30 (NKJV)

I can of Myself do nothing. As I hear, I judge; and My judgment is righteous, because I do not seek My own will but the will of the Father who sent Me.

This is Christ saying "YES" to His Father, this is you saying yes to your Father. Can you see it.

Jesus Live Like this Saints, be intentionally set apart for His use even as He is intentionally set Himself apart for His Father's use. Put yourself in this verse, this is Holiness, meaning "set apart for special use" Are you finally getting the picture, He is our model and our standard. **John 5:30** So we should say, **"I can do nothing on my own, I do not seek my own will but the will of the ONE who sent me."** Do you see that, this verse is written just for You insert yourself?

The Bible is written for you. [Narcissistic behavior lifts oneself up. I am telling you to become a zero with the rim rubbed out. I am suggesting you go down to be the servant of all, become a child in simple dependency and trust upon God in all things, pick up your cross and think of others as greater importance than yourself. This is NOT Narcissistic]

John15:4-5 (NKJV)

4 Abide in Me, and I in you. As the branch cannot bear fruit of itself, unless it abides in the vine, neither can you, unless you abide in Me.

5 "I am the vine, you are the branches. He who abides in Me, and I in him, bears much fruit; for without Me you can do nothing.

So, we are here abiding, living dependent, relying like a child upon Jesus through the Spirit bearing His fruit. This is why all the Glory goes to Jesus because we give Him away and not ourselves. The fruit we bear is from the seed He gave us. He is the author the one source and provider of all thing we are vessel of obedience He is the finisher that gets the Glory for what He has been done through us. Don't touch the glory. Throw down your crown; it all belongs to Him.

Philippians 4:13 (NKJV)

¹³ I can do all things through Christ who strengthens me.

With Him we can live and thrive rightly in Him with an awaken conscience focused not to grieve the spirit that lives in us. In Him, we have our victory.

Amos 3:3 (NKJV)

Can two walk together, unless they be agreed?

We need to learn to walk in agreement with Christ meaning in agreement with His word and spirit. This is how we walk hand in hand together with Him. We input His word into our minds, now it is turned into a filter of how I see the life God has given me. My responsibility is to respond as the word filter suggests this is how we say "yes" to God. When my wife and I walk hand in hand, one of us is walking and the other is following. When we do this with Christ, He leads, we follow. **John 10:27**, in unity with Him and His purposes taught to us through the word of truth that we have studied and understood. Walk hand in hand in submission with Him Saints! But to walk in Christ's love, it will cost you your own self-nature: Deny your self-nature take up your cross and Follow Him. Lay down your own ways and pick up His ways. Lay down your own thinking and pick up His thinking. Lay down your own rightness and Love one another with mercy and grace then give them the truth that sets men free to all He has given you. **Hosea 6:6.**

I have had, to the shame of the church, pastors tell me that not everyone will study and the word. I tell them if we as leaders do not hold up the standard of holiness the inner court life then they will never reach for it. What do they say on in handgun training? You will always hit at what you are not aiming for. Or the reverse you will hit what you aim at. Jesus the firstborn of many brethren read **Romans 8:29 (NKJV)**

Isaiah 41:13 (NKJV)

For I, the Lord your God, will hold your right hand, saying to you, 'Fear not, I will help you."

This reveals our walk we can be hand and hand with Him showing intimacy, agreement in direction and purpose with a deeper trust building friendship with Him leading desiring His heart over our own. I walk hand in hand with my grandchildren and wife today I wish with my kids. How about you? When I walk hand in hand today there is a trust-building effort working between us with every step, have you ever noticed? When I do ministry and I ask for your hand and you give it to me and this opens the heart of the recipient, love is flowing to receive what God may have for them. Loving trust opens hearts to receive, have you ever observed the power of touch?

2 Corinthians 5:18 (NKJV)

18 And all things are of God, who hath reconciled us to himself by Jesus Christ, and hath given to us the ministry of reconciliation;

We are in the reconciliation business with man and God, and man with man. Will you think and live this way saints? Critics and gossips are not allowed. Jesus could not carry offense and carry the cross at the same time and neither should we. If we hold offense, we expose a crack in our armor and Satan will exploit that crack and sneak in and corrupt you without fail. Hold no account or bitterness to anyone because of unfair lose in your life I have seen this so so many times in my own life, hold life with all its stuff with your palm open, never grip it.**1 John 2:10, Romans 16:17, Ephesians 4:31 (AMP)**

Live Like Christ

Philippians 1:10 (NKJV)

¹⁰ that you may approve the things that are excellent, that you may be sincere and without offense till the day of Christ,

I choose to live not being offended when I have been miss treated by others but I prefer to sow in grace and mercy because I need to reap it in my own life. I choose rather to have the fruit of self-control and to offer grace to others that I may reap the same from God. Christ did this for me, so I do the same for others. I am a work in progress I can love folks while they are rejecting me to my face just like Christ did, it is difficult. When possible, I try not to render opinions that easily cause offence and lead to sin, my goal is not give or take offense. I pursue Christ and speak the truth in Love. **Matthew 18:7.**

Some might say, "me too," I stand for truth and if the world does not like it, too bad. Does that work with your wife, I ask? I am not sure that Christ Jesus Lived this way. Truth without love is a harsh hammer. Maybe to the religious folks like some Christian critics that have pop up even today. The unbelievers have never given me the grief, like the religious folks do, that is interesting. Satan's work is just like it was in Jesus's day, religious folks being critics and dividers more than the unbelievers. I will error on the side of love, love for my enemies the Lord commands. Jesus is saying He loved the Pharisees but spiritual ignorance influenced by demons were the true enemies of Christ and I will do the same. Our fight is not with flesh and blood, with Pharisees, or religious critics of today but I can win through Love that over-looks a fault and never fails. Error, blindness or ignorance of others is overlooked for the sake of the kingdom to win them to Christ. Love is the soil conditioner to the seed of Life for eternal truth to take root and change the Hearts of MEN.

I Peter 4:8 (AMP)

Above all things, have intense unfailing Love for one another, for Love covers a multitude of sins forgives and disregards the offenses of others.

If God is telling us to live this way in this verse can we assume that He also lived this way with us? He loves and covers our sins for the sake of being able to train us when we are close to Him. Have you ever noticed with your walk with God, it is not about Christ being correct about a doctrine or thing? It is always about maintaining the opportunity to train you once more again and again the relationship is the focus. It is always your choice to yield to Him, pick up your cross and follow Him. He seeks like a husband to a wife to keep her close that he may salt and re-salt her again and again. His relationship with Her is more important, love is more important than truth telling, truth will come but love must be first. Speak the truth in love. With an everlasting love and kindness, I will draw thee to truth say God in **Jeremiah 31:3**. Do you see it brother?

Jesus ignored your SIN and drew you close with mercy and grace then you found and understood His love and you chose Him, then salvation came even though you still had SIN in your life. Truth won through love, right? Then little by little He, the Spirit works out the sin in you, His washing of the word of truth cleanses you over time, right? Have you sinned recently and Jesus did not kick you to the curb because of it? He allows your sinful self to seek Him again and again. Think on this.

So do the same with everyone one God has given you. Prefer the relationship vs being right about a topic or thing, so that you may speak into the life of that person delivering grace and mercy over and over salt and re-salt water and re-water. A walk like this, woos folks unto salvation, restoration and the renewing of the mind. It is the work of **Jeremiah 31:3**. Read it.

Fathers, mothers, and friends **they need the Jesus in you**. They need to see you overlook their sins just as Christ overlooked your sins. O no…. **Your kids and neighbors need to know you will love them even though they have failed you and failed God?** God gave you to your lost folks around you for you to speak into their life so that Christ may take root in them on good love conditioned, forgiven soil. Christ did this for the twelve He chose, He also did it for you, modeling to us to do it to others as well. The goal is Christ in them, the hope of glory, the change that is everlasting, Jesus the mighty and glorious one's seed that changes hearts of men that they may know heaven's King. He makes sinners, wicked murderers like Paul into saints whose seeds is still bearing fruit today. Jesus's seed, via Paul, is still bringing the gospel fruit into the Gentiles world even today. Think about how many have eaten the fruit of the seed planted in the disciples' hearts for Christ today because of love.

Proverbs 10:12 (AMP)

Hatred stirs up strife [division], But love covers and overwhelms all transgressions [forgiving and overlooking another's faults].

Hate towards people is from the tree of good and evil and its fruit kills and destroys. Do you want to live like this verse above, Christ did, will you follow Him? Do you want to sow this into others so that you may reap it as well? How much forgiveness do you need? Then SOW it, plant it, and give it to others in the same measure saints you will reap. Be fruitful!

James 3:17 (NKJV)

17 But the wisdom that is from above is first pure, then peaceable, gentle, willing to yield to God and to the brethren, full of mercy and good fruits, without partiality and without hypocrisy.

Is this teaching able to yield good fruit in you, peaceable and pure because of love that is in it? Are you willing to think and live like this? Christ did, pick up your cross, and deny yourself and follow Him! Do not live your life one more moment your own way, live it His way! How much mercy and grace do I give out to my brothers in this world? God is not mocked in the same measure you will reap. Read **Galatians 6:7,** and if you sow judgement, look out, you will reap the same.

Something to Ponder

Jesus spoke to five thousand people all at once and taught them holy thinking and taught them the truth of the Kingdom. In His teaching they discover their own sinfulness by Christ teaching of holiness. An example is the Beatitudes. The miracle is in the mirror the word of truth that reveals and reflects back to us my own sinful brokenness and our need for Him. Do you understand this?

To bring everlasting change into their lives, He lifted a truth standard, holiness. When we train folks how to think His way this is the good fruit for others to pick from, that results in repentance, a change of thinking working in them, this is the holy walk called the WAY. "For as a man thinks in his heart so is he" in his actions. The Bible is true and Jesus is Our Father's expression of HIS love and truth and our sample Son for us to model after in this world. So love one-anther and model the pattern SON Jesus. Jesus teaches us through the word of truth to be holy, to study what is Good to seek out His face. Just like **Psalms 1 and 119**. This changes our thinking which results in a better you. A holy you, a set apart for His Use, YOU. It is all about YOU, do you see it.

Matthew 9:11 (NKJV)

And when the Pharisees saw it, they said to His disciples, "Why does your Teacher eat with tax collectors and sinners?

Do you think Jesus sat and eat with sinners of whatever category and pointed out their sins in front of others embarrassing them with truth and breaking His own rule to correct individuals one on one? He sat down and did the same thing that He did when He spoke to those on the mount. He spoke in favor of Holiness vs against SIN, He lifted a standard to live unto. Is it better to have a sign on the freeway that says, "you sinners are going to Hell, repent" or a sign that says, "Please, everyone come to me and know me better, said Jesus and as you do come to Him you will let go of your favorite sinful ways?" Jesus said to compel them to come to the wedding. That means, using drawing tools like love and care vs a hammer or sword to bring them in, always allowing choice because here is when God is in the mix. Convince, persuade, dispel someone's doubts with kindness and love, this works well in a one-on-one settings. The spirit will finish the work of sanctification, and cleansing of Sin, it has never been the pastors Job to clean the people in the church. Do not compromise the word of God in any way but always point people to Christ and His ways of thinking. Teach them "how to" get into His presence and read, learn the word of wisdom and always speak the truth in Love. We are created inside of us, to want Him, even more of Him, just present Him, hunger for Him, remember it is better "felt than telt." You can't lead folks to places you have not been, you heard me right. Same with worship leaders, you can take folks into His presence of God if you have not been there yourself on your own!

Think on this, the more I make Jesus the answer to my every question, the more I seek Him and give Him away, the better the world and the folks around me benefit from my overflow of HIM. This is the walk of faith a dependent posture upon Him, to give Him away, to be a sign post pointing folks to Him. He is the source the fount and the abundant life flows from Him. They get some of God overflowing of my cup and touching them making them hungry for Him the source the answer is Jesus. People that live from here are the ones that turn the world upside down, try it.

Teach people Holy thinking and they will willingly give up their sins to adore the King. This is so irritating to me to see but turn up the lights and encourage folks to bring their Bibles and notebooks teach them how to study and learn from it. Something I learned from God. A "C" student brings their textbook to class because they are told to, and never open them at home. An "A" student brings a textbook, notebook, and pencil taught to be ready to learn with open hearts, hungry for Him and His word and uses his Bible at home to discover and go deeper what he learned at church. My job is to make people **passionate** about the word of God and to become an "A" student, if you will. While in leadership roles, I Teach folks to LOVE God and His word. To desire to eat from the Tree of Life and teach them how to navigate the textbook of life, the Bible, the word is our owner's manual to abundant life.

Encourage note taking, and highlighting your Bible so you can share it with others away from church and with yourself in your own study times. Don't we, as pastors, want our members or students to be contagious about the word of God and their Love for Christ? Our job is to equip them and model it for them so they can do the same to others. When I teach, bring your Bibles, notebooks, and highlighters. Turn up the lights you will know with understand your Bible the word of abundant life better. The more you know the Bible, the more you know Christ and in Him is the fullness of joy. Is that exactly what we want to create in folks the love for God and teach others to do the same again and again. This is the first commandment: LOVE GOD. Let's restore relationships between God and man and teach them how to do it. Leaders need to be contagious about their love for God and His word because it is better felt than told to desire the presence of the King. Teach them How. His word, and presence we need so desperately in this church world today. If your passion for Him ends with you, you have become a stagnant pond vs being a river of living water touching many banks and creating change in those banks as you flow down river. Ponder this and teach them How to love God first then love man second.

Proverbs 23:7a (NKJV)

For as a man thinks in his heart, so is he…

If you have lasted this long through the lesson and the seed has fallen on to good ground, in your heart? You now understand God's love for man and our responsibility to love others as He loved us because of God's Scriptures taught here. The seed is in your heart now and it is time to water it to enable it to grow. Feed it, get into prayer and worship times with Him, study times with Him love on Jesus and love His people. Know this, as you enter this life with Christ, He will change the hearts of men through the spirit to those He has given you. Our responsibility is to sow good seed on good ground and water it duplicating what He has done in us in others. Abiding in Him is the only way to bear much fruit saints.

His Love is not earned [grace], it is freely given even to the undeserving then we ought to do the same to others, your love must be freely given and not earned. Quickly SOW it in others' lives!

His Law is LOVE, sow it in others and His gospel is peace, sow it in others.

His truth is hidden in Him and revealed in the seeking of Him, sow the hunger in others, model it in others, water it in others, give it away, too others that you may reap the same. Leave this earth and the people around you better than you found them.

My Prayer for you is this verse

Philippians 1:9-11 (NKJV)

9 And this I pray, that your love may abound still more and more in knowledge and all discernment, 10 that you may approve the things that are excellent, that you may be sincere and without offense till the day of Christ, 11 being filled with the fruits of righteousness which are by Jesus Christ, to the glory and praise of God.

Jeremiah 31:3-4, Ephesians 4:32, Romans 13:8

My friends, these are lessons of the heart I had to learn myself, because of my own pride and own mistakes in my own life I now have set them apart for you and others like you to eat from.

Jesus is the secret being revealed in you, He is becoming the key to your every locked door. This is why we sing "HOLY HOLY HOLY" because our reaction in discovering that He was always the answer, accept Him as truth leading you unto Salvation and Holy understanding and thinking of who He is.

Remember to yield to Him every day in prayer, being still in His presence and the study of His word because **For as a man thinks in his heart so is he** in his actions, do. **Psalms 1 and 119.**

Blessings to you.

Be a Peace Maker Saints,
Edward Morales

As a Man Thinks in His Heart So is He

Contact us at:
Edward L. Morales
EdwardLMorales@outlook.com

Milton Keynes UK
Ingram Content Group UK Ltd.
UKHW010710050224
437294UK00018B/727